LIBERTARIANISM

For and Against

Craig Duncan and Tibor R. Machan

ROWMAN & LITTLEFIELD PUBLISHERS, INC.
Lanham • Boulder • New York • Toronto • Oxford

ROWMAN & LITTLEFIELD PUBLISHERS, INC

Published in the United States of America
by Rowman & Littlefield Publishers, Inc.
A wholly owned subsidary of The Rowman & Littlefield Publishing
Group, Inc.
4501 Forbes Boulevard, Suite 200, Lanham, Maryland 20706
www.rowmanlittlefield.com

PO Box 317
Oxford
OX2 9RU, UK

British Library Cataloguing in Publication Information Available

Library of Congress Cataloging-in-Publication Data

Duncan, Craig, 1969–
    Libertarianism : for and against / Craig Duncan and Tibor R. Machan.
        p. cm.
    Includes bibliographical references and index.
    ISBN 0-7425-4258-0 (cloth : alk. paper) — ISBN 0-7425-4259-9 (pbk. : alk.
    paper)
    1. Libertarianism. 2. Liberalism. I. Machan, Tibor R. II. Title.

JC585.D83 2005
320.51'2—dc22   2004027526

Printed in the United States of America

♾™ The paper used in this publication meets the minimum requirements
of American National Standard for Information Sciences—Permanence of
Paper for Printed Library Materials, ANSI/NISO Z39.48-1992.

For Trena—CD

For the Dougs—TRM

Contents

PART II

Foreword

Martha C. Nussbaum

The topic addressed in this book is of extraordinary importance. In the world as a whole, inequalities in basic welfare and life chances are rapidly growing. As the United Nations Development Program summarized the situation in its *Human Development Report 2000*:

> Global inequalities in income increased in the 20th century by orders of magnitude out of proportion to anything experienced before. The distance between the incomes of the richest and poorest country was about 3 to 1 in 1820, 35 to 1 in 1950, 44 to 1 in 1973 and 72 to 1 in 1992.

People of good will in wealthy nations naturally wonder what ethical responsibility, if any at all, they bear for changing this situation and whether such problems are best addressed through private charity or through government action, or through some combination of the two.

Within the United States too inequality is a daily fact of life. From now on let us focus simply on the issue of inequality within a single nation. About one fifth of America's children live in poverty, and the absence of national health care means that many children and adults go without the opportunity for basic medical treatment. Although the United States is among the richest nations in the world in terms of gross domestic product per capita,[1] it does not do so well on other social indicators. Twenty-six nations rank ahead of the United States in life expectancy (including some relatively poor nations, such as Costa Rica and Barbados). If we look at the probability at birth of not surviving to age sixty, the U.S. figure is 12.6 percent, whereas most European nations are around 8 percent. Maternal mortality is another area in which the United States lags behind others.

One reason for the poor performance of the United States in these areas is surely the fact that it has much more inequality than most developed countries, and this translates into lack of opportunity for many people to get adequate health care and to lead safe and healthy lives. On the so-called Gini Index, a measure of economic inequality commonly used by economists, the United States has greater inequality than any nation in Europe and Australasia, much more inequality than Canada, and around the same amount as Hong Kong and Singapore. To put it another way, the richest 10 percent in the United States have 15.9 times as much income as the poorest 10 percent. Given the absence of national health care, poverty usually means inadequate prenatal care and lack of essential medicines and treatments for children. Nobel Prize–winning economist Amartya Sen has demonstrated that the life expectancy and health data for Harlem in New York City are very similar to those for Kerala in southern India, a poor state in one of the world's poorer countries. Such data suggest that the gap left by the absence of state action in these areas has not been made up by effective private action, not where poorer Americans are concerned. The wealth generated by permitting high rates of inequality does not exactly "trickle down" to the poor, at least not enough to give all children a decent shot at life.

If one believes, as I do, that all human beings ought to have opportunities for lives in accordance with human dignity, these are depressing statistics. There have also been, however, some encouraging signs in the United States over the past few decades. One of the most encouraging is in the area of disability. We have done much more than most nations to integrate people with a variety of physical and mental impairments into the educational system, the work force, and generally into full participation in social life. If one were to measure the life opportunities for people with a variety of disabilities, the United States would rank well. But how has this development come about? The state, with laws such as the Americans with Disabilities Act and the Individuals with Disabilities Education Act, has taken a strong hand. Such strong state measures are increasingly under threat, in a nation in which libertarian thought increasingly holds sway.

Libertarianism is an old political movement; it has been around in some form ever since the 1960s. In some form, such ideas are probably much older; at least, their proponents trace them to (their interpretations of) much older thinkers, such as John Locke in the seventeenth century. But in the Reagan/ Thatcher era and since, libertarian ideas have taken on increasing importance in the public debate. By now it is not at all uncommon for people to assume that taxation is a morally problematic interference with property that is theirs, and to which they have a right; that a strong state is bound to be a tyrant, playing havoc with people's freedoms; that such measures as laws protecting people with disabilities, laws making sexual harassment in the workplace illegal, and laws protecting the environment are all excesses of overweening state power. Many Americans feel that we would be better off if the state just "kept its hands off" the parts of life that people value most.

Now, of course, there is general agreement that the state has the obligation to protect national security and to protect all citizens from force and fraud; to maintain systems of contract and property rights; to ensure, in general, that the rule of law prevails over anarchy. Anyone who ponders these areas of life will see that personal freedom does not mean the absence of state action. If the police, the fire department, the legal system, and the military do not do their jobs, nobody is particularly free. But beyond this point there is great disagreement. People disagree about taxation—who has a right to what, and what is a reasonable tax structure. They differ about anti-discrimination laws, libertarians typically holding that they are a bad thing but many other Americans holding that they are essential to a society that values racial justice, gender justice, and justice for people with disabilities. They differ about environmental protection, some holding that industry should be free to make any choice that seems profitable, others holding that state protection of the environment contributes to the well-being of all.

Both sides ought to agree, however, that the choices we make in this matter are complex. There is no option of simply "letting" everyone be "free" through "state inaction." If one lives (as I have for periods of time, in rural India) in a place that has no clean water supply, no electricity, no public transportation, no public education, and no reliable legal system, one will discover that one is not very free there to do the things one wants to do. We should all agree that any meaningful human freedom requires the state to provide some essential services and guarantees. Moreover, in a rich nation such as the United States, the choice to leave these matters unattended to is not inaction but a choice; it is action. The differences between sides must concern the extent and the nature of various state protections, and the nature of the actions the state should choose.

The debates that typically go on over such matters in American politics are hasty and strident. They employ "sound bites" and slogans rather than reasoned arguments. But democracy requires something better of us all—it requires that we really think through our choices and stand for what we can defend with good arguments. To make good arguments, we also need to listen to the arguments of others. Often two sides in a debate share important assumptions, and progress can be made simply by setting out the argument in detail and finding out where the differences really are. There has been a long tradition of argument, in Western philosophy, about the scope of state authority; thus listening well in this area means listening as well to the arguments that predecessors have made.

The aim of the exchange between Machan and Duncan is to provide an example of reasoned philosophical debate on these important issues. Machan and Duncan differ sharply about what is right in this area, but both agree in their commitment to reason. They lay out their positions with admirable clarity, so that the reader can see where they agree (on the importance of human dignity, for example) and where they disagree. The structure of the book is like that of a philosophical dialogue, each one posing questions and replying to the questions the other has posed.

We can all learn by constantly confronting the best arguments on the other side of the questions we care about, as well as the arguments that support our own positions. My foreword has not been at all neutral, and I do not intend it to be. I have suggested some reasons why I am strongly skeptical about libertarian thought. But this means that I owe it to myself to (re)read and ponder the arguments of Machan even more than those of Duncan, and to try to think what the best arguments are for the position that I have previously rejected. I hope that readers who come to this book with strongly held positions on one side of this debate will focus on learning the arguments on the other. That is not only a good thing for one's arguments, it is a good thing for mutual respect in a democratic society.

Note

1. The only nations that rank ahead of the United States in the data of the 2004 *Human Development Report* are Norway, Ireland, and Luxembourg.

Acknowledgments

Craig Duncan would first like to thank Tibor Machan for being such a civil and amiable debate partner, despite the depth of disagreement between us. Thanks are due too to the editors of the *Philosophers' Magazine* for publishing the "Open Debate" on libertarianism (First and Third Quarters 2003) out of which this project grew. Special thanks go as well to Peter Bardaglio, provost of Ithaca College, for arranging (with very short notice) a faculty summer research grant, which was crucial to the completion of this project. After a draft of my chapters was completed, the comments of my colleagues Stephen Schwartz, Frederick Kaufman, and Sean McKeever led to many improvements and were much appreciated. Finally, I am grateful to my wife Trena Haffenden, whose support sustains me, and to our children Joseph and Beth, who have taught me as much about responsibility as I have them.

Tibor Machan, in turn, wishes to thank Craig Duncan for proposing this exciting project and for handling much of the red tape associated with it, as well as for the civil tone of his side of the discussion. He is also grateful to the *Philosophers' Magazine* for hosting the initial debate on libertarianism. Jim Chesher, Tibor's longtime friend and his coauthor for several books, has been very generous with his time and skill as he provided suggestions and some criticism of Tibor's portion of the input in this debate. Chapman University and Freedom Communications, Inc., should also be thanked for the support Tibor has received for working on this project. Of course, the content of his contributions are entirely his responsibility.

Finally, both authors would like to thank Eve DeVaro and Melissa McNitt of Rowman and Littlefield for their able assistance with this project.

A Note to Readers

Not just American but world politics often revolves around which conception of justice—or of a good society—should be the aim not only of politicians and public officials but (especially) of citizens. Much of the globe is at this time grappling with the challenges of citizenship participation. The more citizens get involved and the better educated they become, the more their input—or their act of withholding it—will influence the nature of the polities in which they live.

Of course, this assumes something about which philosophers and others debate a good deal: Are we really in control of our lives, particularly our political fates? We will not, however, enter that important discussion in this book, assuming instead that what people think and do does make a difference, even if slowly, on the shapes their societies are to take. In our case, we urge two different ideals about this matter.

Tibor Machan is convinced that the libertarian idea of justice is right and ought to be promoted and implemented wherever that is possible, while Craig Duncan advocates democratic liberalism. These two positions may not seem to be in opposition, and in some contexts of political discussion their differences are not especially significant.

Critiques of Western democracies often encompass both positions involved in our debate. But once the broad framework of Western democracies is embraced, there remain serious questions about exactly what kinds of constitutional provisions should be laid down and developed into the various nuances of a country's legal order.

Machan holds that a certain idea of individual rights should constitute the centerpiece of a society's system of justice, worked out within its system of law. He argues for the view that an extension of John Locke's theory of individual rights to one's life and property—in Locke, "person" and "estate"—is required for a just society. Duncan, in contrast, holds that a democratic liberal system ought to develop into a polity the constitution of which provides for all a measure of security and well-being, via public policy. Thus some redistribution of wealth, where it is required for providing such security and well-being, is an imperative of justice as Duncan sees it.

Since this is a debate-format book involving two authors with very opposed ideas, some words are in order regarding the process of writing the book. As the first step, each author composed—independently of the other—an essay outlining and defending his political philosophy. These first essays respectively constitute chapter 1 (Machan's defense of libertarianism) and chapter 4 (Duncan's defense of democratic liberalism) of the book. After completing these opening essays defending their philosophies, the authors exchanged them with each other, and each author then penned a critique of the other's opening essay. These critiques, also written independently of each other, became chapters 2 (Duncan's critique of libertarianism) and 5 (Machan's critique of democratic liberalism). Finally, the critiques were exchanged, and each author wrote a rebuttal; the rebuttals are chapters 3 and 6.

After completing the chapters, some light editing was done to polish the prose, but the substance was left in place, so that neither author could retroactively change points that his coauthor criticizes in later chapters. After all, such retroactive changes are impossible in a live debate, and the goal throughout was to simulate the structure of a live debate insofar as possible, thereby capturing some of the dynamism of that format. The resulting back-and-forth, we think, cuts to the heart of this important debate and reveals how a civil exchange of objections and replies can illuminate a topic that so often generates shouting matches. As for which side prevails in this reasoned exchange, we leave that to you, the reader, to judge.

PART I

1

The Case for Libertarianism: Sovereign Individuals

Tibor R. Machan

What I wish to argue here is that libertarianism, as the development of classical liberalism and the political principles sketched in the American Declaration of Independence, is the best answer to the question, "How ought we to organize our political societies?" Since the Declaration is an announcement, not a detailed treatise, this concise statement of political ideals needs to be fleshed out. The bottom line, though, of the Founders' idea, as well as of libertarianism, is that individual members of human communities are sovereign, self-ruling or self-governing, agents whose sovereignty any just system of laws must accommodate.[1]

Throughout the world, the thinking about the United States by ordinary folks—or at least in terms of the United States as a political community—still brings to mind the substance expressed in the Declaration. This is that people have been created equal and endowed by their creator—be that God or nature—with unalienable rights, and that the role of government in a just system is to "secure these rights."

The revolutionary element in the Declaration is that unlike in most official political statements of the past, it deems the individuals constituting society to be the focus of political importance—not the monarch, chief, tribe, party, class, or even majority. The reference to unalienability renders the document an especially radical one. It affirms the uncompromising priority, within the context of public-policy decision making, of everyone's rights—among others, those to life, liberty, and the pursuit of happiness. It also assigns to the just powers of governments the primary function of securing these rights. Thus the Declaration of Independence is *in its essence* a libertarian document—it is concerned with the basic right to individual liberty of all those who are citizens of a political community.[2]

Libertarianism—once referred to as "classical liberalism"—proposes a strictly limited conception of politics, in contrast to that embodied in, for example, monarchies (from absolute types to those limited by the parliament), the welfare state, fascism, or socialism. All such latter systems have top-down structures and hierarchies of importance, in which certain common ends or goals—or as the late Robert Nozick called them, "end states"—are sought for everyone, rather than the bottom-up type envisioned by the American founders, which stresses *procedural* principles by which the society is to be governed. Order, fairness, cultural superiority, and the like are not the goals of "bottom-up" governance; consensual community life is.

It is human individuals, living their lives on terms of their own, who matter most in such a political system. Even the much championed democratic aspect of such a system is strictly limited. The method of democratic decision making is to be circumscribed and restricted so that only those democratic decisions can be construed as just and proper that do not violate individual rights.

As a matter of history, the U.S. Constitution gave some, although by no means full, expression of the ideals stated in the Declaration. There were some major contradictions, including slavery and some other coercive features within the Constitution, supposedly allowed so as to appease some powerful prospective U.S. citizens for the sake of creating a strong federal union that would be capable of resisting foreign intervention. Still, what has been perceived as particularly novel about the American founders' vision remains a serious political alternative today and still energizes a great many people to seek to emigrate to the United States so they may benefit from the protection of individual human rights promised, albeit somewhat confusedly, in that society.

What specifically are these energizing ideals? What does the claim mean that every adult individual has unalienable rights—rights that cannot be lost so long as one remains a human being—to, among other things, life, liberty, and the pursuit of happiness? That claim translates into a system of political society wherein everyone is authorized to carry on his or her chosen activities and pursue his or her objectives, only if doing so does not violate others' rights—and wherein the government's role is restricted, as already noted, to securing these individual rights. Other valued goals and ends are to be sought without the use of coercive force, even that which government might lend in aid of such pursuits. There is an underlying assumption in the Declaration and in libertarianism that once human beings are forbidden to deploy coercive force in pursuit of their objectives, they will tend to pursue them peacefully, with one another's consent, and that this will produce as good a human community as is achievable among human beings. Indeed, libertarianism stresses the ideal of civil society—meaning a society that eschews dealing with one another by subjugation, oppression, conquest, or similar coercive means, means taken to be standard in the non-human animal world.

It is worth noting here, parenthetically, that among libertarian political philosophers and theorists it is generally understood that there is a decisive difference between *coercion* and *force*—the former is initiated, unjustified, and oppressive, whereas the latter is the application of physical power for various purposes, some of which can be quite justified, such as self-defense or the defense of someone who has delegated this authority to another, or, of course, various productive ends, such as hauling bricks or moving boulders. Force is akin to violence, which may be justified or not. Thus, being forced to work may be unobjectionable if the source of this force is the necessity to eat.[3] (Not all libertarian thinkers keep strictly to the distinction—some will use the phrase "coercive force" to indicate the difference involved.)

One way to see this is to understand government as having the professional duty to protect the basic rights of the citizenry that has instituted, "hired," or established it. This is probably fruitfully illustrated by how at a sports event referees are hired to carry out a strictly limited role, namely, to make sure everyone plays by the rules of the game.[4] (Just as referees can come to the aid of injured athletes without their job description being changed to "medics," so government officials are not barred from occasionally answering to emergencies. The cop on the beat, though a peacekeeper, may now and then give directions to someone who is lost, provided this does not interfere with his essential task.)

Government's role, like the referee's, is important, without doubt. The institution has been perceived as important, despite much of the malpractice of various governments over the centuries, because it is reasonably well understood that in human affairs it is necessary and valuable to uphold standards of conduct and have specialists to do so properly, adhering to the complications of due process. This is to say that justice must be secured justly. (For libertarians the debate concerns mostly whether a government, with a monopoly over the lawful use of force within some region, or whether various "defense-insurance"—or justice—agencies, without any such monopoly status, ought to carry out this task.[5] Some libertarian theorists call themselves "anarchists," some "minarchists." The former substitute for government what they call defense-insurance agencies, competing legal services or the like, whereas the latter argue for a noncoercive system of law enforcement that would amount to proper government, via the full—explicit or implicit—consent of the governed, yet that would be a natural monopoly within a given geographical region.)

But politicians and bureaucrats, with the precarious task of securing our rights without violating them as they do so, are not also doctors, dentists, dance instructors, or members of some other profession. Professional referees do some very specific things, primarily to adjudicate disputes over rules—and that is essentially what the libertarian or classical liberal political position proposes. It rests on the idea that once they reach adulthood human beings are sovereign individuals, with no proper authority to govern another without that other's consent to be governed. As Abraham Lincoln put the point, "No man is good enough to govern another man, without that other's consent."[6] Any coercion by one person of another is thus deemed unjustified, and government is employed to protect everyone against such coercion, including itself. (Force used defensively or in retaliation is not, as we have seen, the same as coercion—the use of force in violation of people's rights—although the distinction is not often put in these terms.)

The mainstream political stance, in contrast, tends to be represented by advocates of a more or less expanded welfare state, both those on the Left and on the Right. What mainstream politicians argue over are the expenses—and at times the scope—of a democratically guided coercive welfare state, not whether such a state should exist or is just.

I say "coercive," but this begs the question, since advocates of the welfare state often hold that what is taken from a person, be it assets or labor time, is in fact owed to others by a natural obligation of some sort, that others have a positive right to it. If, for example, Charles Taylor is correct that we belong to our communities, that we are a part of these communities, then the services and resources we are made to contribute are like dues we owe. As Taylor laments, "Theories which assert the primacy of rights are those which take as the fundamental, or at least a fundamental, principle of their political theory the ascription of certain rights to individuals which deny the same status to a principle of belonging or obligation, that is a principle which states our obligation as men to belong to or sustain society, or a society of a certain type, or to obey authority or an authority of a certain type."[7]

I have argued elsewhere, however, that rights theories in the Lockean tradition do not take rights to have normative primacy. Rights are derived from the requirements of the ethics of individual flourishing within the context of human communities. There is no denial of the essential sociality of human beings, but the Lockean tradition maintains that the individual needs to be at liberty to determine to what sort of community he or she will belong—if only by means of tacit or implicit consent—and that the right kind is one in which his or her sovereignty has primacy. It is only such a community that is fitting—that is, meets the standard of justice—for human beings.

Libertarians, following the political vision of the American founders (who themselves took their cues from the likes of John Locke), believe that people have to take care of their own specific welfare, within and by the voluntary cooperation of their various communities and associations—families, churches, service organizations, companies, clubs, and so on. Only the *general* welfare is to be promoted by government,[8] the securing of our basic rights—just as referees may be said to promote the general welfare of an athletic event by upholding its rules. People, in turn, are capable of doing their job of promoting their specific welfare—pursuing their own happiness—effectively if the government sticks to this refereeing role, namely, running the courts, the police, and the country's defense.

Obviously, there are nuances and complications when one translates these libertarian ideals into practical policy. Still it is fairly clear that libertarian political thinking would contrast sharply with a great deal of the current mainstream thinking in even the Western world, let alone the rest of the world, concerning the purpose of politics.

Interestingly enough, in the international arena the language of this libertarian classical liberal political position is vibrant now. Ideas such as privatization, globalization, property rights, and the infrastructure of a free market system concern the extension throughout the world of the ideas laid out in the U.S. Declaration of Independence. If the people of all the various societies around the globe want to prosper and improve their lives, they do better by adopting the principles of a free society associated with the American political tradition than those of competing systems. Although in the United States such ideals are not fully embraced or manifest, there remains throughout the world a rhetorical identification of America with the ideals of a fully free, voluntarist society of civil liberties, freedom of thought and worship, free trade, free markets, and capitalism. It is these ideas that are exported in the movement roughly identified as "globalization."

Also, interestingly, when the foreign policies of the U.S. government are evaluated, libertarian notions tend to appear—such as the critique of preemptive military attack, which rests, at least implicitly, on the idea that unless someone initiates force against a country—or is about to do so—that country is not authorized to take forcible action. In short, the idea that force must be limited to self-defense is quite prominent in such discussions, yet of course many abandon it when it comes to the role they assign to government in domestic affairs (e.g., precautionary government regulations of various professions, which arguably violate the ban on prior restraint, the prohibition of using force on those who have not violated anyone's rights but merely *might* do so).

Now, what is crucial is why this libertarian alternative is a good idea. It is one thing to say "We're for it" but another thing to say "We're for it because it's right." In a column in *The New Republic,* the author once recalled having attended an economic conference in Japan and being cornered by a Japanese official who complained that the Americans are arrogant because they try to implore everybody else to accept their views about markets and economies. Certainly libertarians do this as well.

Of course, nearly all political ideals are championed for all, although in recent times the doctrine of multiculturalism has tended to soften that stance.[9] One way of putting the point is to ask, "Why should what was laid out for Americans work elsewhere or be right for others around the globe? Why can't different communities have their own different political systems?" Many people say that about Cuba or even North Korea and (before March 2003) Iraq—why should these change into more democratic, individualist societies rather than stick to their more collectivist systems? Maybe within those societies such a system is more suitable. Yet, of course, those societies too are championed by some who would wish the whole world conformed to their visions. So the problem of proposing political ideas across the board, for all human communities, faces not only libertarians. If the implicit notion that liberation is a kind of imperialism made good sense here, one could go on to argue that urging Cuba, Iran, or any other society around the globe to "democratize"—on the American, classical liberal model—would be to practice imperialism, of attempting to impose on others a system that is suited not to them but only to the society imploring them to change. It would smack of empire building, making every society conform to the principles of a dominant one. That is just the complaint some make about American-style Western liberalism as well as its purified version, libertarianism.

Yet, advocating everyone's basic right to negative liberty— that is, liberty from others' intrusive or aggressive conduct— and trying to export it peacefully, by persuasion and economic pressures, imposes nothing on anybody (just as a strike by workers does not constitute a coercive imposition on anyone). Yes, an idea and policies consistent with it are being advocated, suggested, and recommended. But no one is being made to do anything. In fact, the situation is quite the opposite. The libertarian proposal for others to follow is akin to advocating the abolition of slavery. Slave owners looked upon the abolitionists with the same attitude: "Why don't you keep your abolitionism to yourself? We like it here, we have our little quaint tradition called slavery, and you shouldn't come in here and impose upon us your ideas of abolition."[10]

That is the same line that Fidel Castro, Kim Jong Il, and their defenders advance (as Saddam Hussein once did) in response to those who advocate greater democracy and individual rights in the countries they rule: "The Americans are imposing upon us this idea of democracy and individualism when they do not want us to force everyone into collective farming and industrialization." It is the same when others object to free market globalization. What that idea comes to is the freeing up of people's commercial and related activities, the removal of state impediments to them. The people who complain most about it are those who believe they should have the power to run economic institutions, in a top-down fashion, just as monarchies ran their mercantilist societies.

In many corners of the world, this idea that governments are responsible for everything—governments are supposed to establish religions (like in Iran or to some extent even in Israel), governments are supposed to establish the conditions or culture for the arts, for economics, and so on—is still very prominent. Libertarians hold that the American Revolution (and it was a genuine revolution, unlike the Russian one, which was just a change of rulers), had been genuinely radical because it placed on record, officially, for the first time the idea that it is individual human beings who matter most in society, not the tribe, clan, ethnic group, religious organization, or even the family.

Now, libertarianism is sometimes advanced on the grounds that when people enjoy the conditions of negative liberty, everybody makes the best judgments and the most beneficial consequences all around are realized. Such a consequentialist approach is unwise, since it suggests that free men and women always do the right thing while those who would regiment them seldom do. No, libertarianism only requires that everyone ought to be treated as somebody whose judgment matters and who is owed such treatment that his or her own judgment can guide his or her life. Only once this freedom to act on one's judgment is secured can we begin to talk about whether one chooses to do the right thing or the wrong thing, whether one decides correctly or incorrectly. Such a discussion is supposed to be conducted in a civilized fashion, through reason and not coercive force.

In a libertarian system no vice squad is sent to break up prostitution, but prostitutes may be implored to stop their degrading professional practices. Once we send in the vice squad we actually deny the prostitutes their humanity, as if they could not make up their own minds. Indeed, by the libertarian's understanding, any introduction of coercive, initiated force in human relationships does violence to people's humanity. This is because human beings are by their basic nature rational animals, whose primary tool of survival and means of flourishing is thought, for which negative liberty is the central prerequisite. So, even such vital objectives as helping the poor, uneducated, or sick must be achieved not by subduing others and conscripting them to take part in the mission but by convincing them to do so.

There are better ways than coercion to solve problems. The whole point of civilization is to imbue a culture, a society, with the method of reasoning, argument, and persuasion rather than coercive force. Force is supposed to be the major means available to other animals, which do not have the capacity to reason. Humans, in contrast, are supposed to be patient enough to wait until they manage to convince other people or learn to live with the fact that they have not managed that task. That is what is made possible in a system in which rights are the foundation of law.

One of the libertarian elements of the United States of America, one that serves as an instructive model of how a generalization of the position would work, is the guarantee of religious freedom. About 4,200 different religions and denominations range throughout America.[11] Are they at war with each other? They are in a war of words every time one of their members speaks from a pulpit: we are right, our God is right, our scripture is right, and all the other 4,199 sects are wrong. But they do not go to war with each other. They argue. They try to persuade each other.

Why is that possible? One of the reasons is private property rights. They can buy themselves land, build a church, and come together on it; nobody can legally go disturb them there. They have the right to run their own affairs within the confines of what belongs to them. We have that right in a free society, in our backyards, our houses, our yards, our companies, our associations, our clubs, and with our own "stuff." If my stuff really is mine rather than the government's, as some people in our political community believe, then I can assign the use of that stuff either to myself or those to whom I am devoted or some cause I want to support; it is not taken from me by force.

Let me summarize my rather cursorily laid-out points in favor of libertarianism. Human nature consists of everyone's being a rational animal, one whose survival and success depends on initiating the process of thinking about the world, becoming aware, paying attention. In human communities the unique danger that arises is not a matter of the natural obstacles to one's life and success—those one faces in or out of communities. The unique danger is from other persons who would wish to survive and succeed on the basis not of their own efforts or good fortune but of wresting support from other people. So it is sensible, prudent, to establish law and order with the goal of resisting such efforts—criminal undertakings—that impede one's liberty to progress peacefully in life on one's own or with willing others. The right to private property, via property law in developed communities, secures for everyone a sphere of personal jurisdiction so that it can be determined when one is acting within one's own sphere or intrudes on the spheres of others. The job of adjudicating disputes about these "border crossing" matters falls to the legal authorities or government, and they must rectify matters without themselves violating anyone's rights. As far as dealing with other societies is concerned, all this implies that no aggression may be used in international relations and that force may be deployed only in retaliation, whatever internal injustices are perpetrated in other societies.

The crux of libertarianism is, then, individual independence in making decisions, including about associations with others. Ideals such as cultural diversity, economic equality, racial harmony, and the like must not trump this basic value.[12]

Individualism

One source of consternation for many political philosophers and theorists—for example, Karl Marx, C. B. Macpherson, Charles Taylor, Amitai Etzioni, John N. Gray—is the individualist element in classical liberalism and, especially, libertarianism. They have dubbed the version of individualism they associate with these positions "atomistic," meaning that human beings are taken in these views to be isolated, separate, self-sufficient, independent living beings, along the lines of Robinson Crusoe.

It will be useful, therefore, to put on record at least one libertarian view of individualism that refutes this characterization. Individualism is the view that, put briefly, human beings are identifiable as a distinct species in the natural world and have as at least one of their central attributes the capacity to be unique, rational individuals. Whatever else is central about being a human being, each adult person, unless crucially debilitated, has the capacity to govern his or her life by means of the individually initiated process of thought, of conceptual consciousness.[13]

Furthermore, excelling as such an individual human being is the primary, proper goal of each person's life. A just political community, in turn, is one that renders it possible for all (or as many as is realistically possible) to pursue this purpose.

As the novelist-philosopher Ayn Rand put the point—following similar observations by Aristotle and Thomas Aquinas—adult persons are "beings of volitional consciousness." This involves, among other things, the crucial capacity to choose to embark upon—to initiate—a process of (thoughtful) action.

If we are entities of a type that can be a causal agent, an initiator of its own behavior, a crucial basis for individuation arises—that different human beings can and actually do choose to exercise their conscious capacities and direct their ensuing actions differently. Putting it more simply, if we have free will our diverse ways of exercising it can make us each unique. So even if there were nothing else unique about different persons, their free will could introduce an essential individuality into their lives. (This is something with a major impact on the social sciences, on psychology and psychotherapy, and, of course, on ethics and politics.)

Yet different people are also uniquely configured, as it were, as human beings; thus they can face different yet equally vital tasks in their lives. Our fingerprints, voices, shapes, ages, locations, talents, and, most of all, choices are all individuating features, so we are all unique. This is the crux of the individualist thesis. Nonetheless, since we are all such individuals, we constitute one species with a definite nature associated with that species possessed by each member. This may seem paradoxical, that one of the defining attributes of the human (kind of) being is the distinctive potential for individuality, based on both diversity and personal choice.

This position has certain implications that are very close to those usually thought to follow from a somewhat different, often labeled "radical," individualism. These implications are the existence of the libertarian political ideas and ideals of individual rights to life, liberty, and property. We might call the earlier version of individualism "atomistic" or "quantitative," the latter "classical."[14]

Atomistic or radical individualism is distinct. It is usually linked to Thomas Hobbes and his nominalist and moral-subjectivist followers. Its most basic, ontological thesis is that human beings are numerically separate bare particulars (meaning "beings without a nature, without being classifiable as any kind of beings"). Their individuality is quantitative, not qualitative, primarily consisting of their existence as separate entities, not of their capacity and willingness to forge distinctive lives of their own.

A problem that some see with the neo-Hobbesian individualist tradition is that it implies that political norms are ultimately subjective—usually taken to be mere preferences. For Hobbes, to start with, "whatsoever is the object of any man's appetite or desire, that is it which he for his part calleth good: and the object of his hate and aversion, evil." So the classical-liberal polity is itself, by the tenets of such individualism, no more than some people's preference, one that others may not share, and quite legitimately. As some critics have put the point, in terms of the Hobbesian individualist position liberty is just one among many different values people desire. This political tradition has thus been vulnerable to the charge of arbitrariness, of resting simply on preferences that some people—for example, the bourgeoisie, capitalists, or white European males—happen to have.

Even in Hobbes's time there were other versions afoot, usually linked to Christianity. By the tenets of a Christian version, each person is a unique child of God, thus uniquely important and not to be sacrificed to some purpose of the tribe or state, for example.[15] This, at least, is one path to the conclusion that a just political community must make room for the sovereignty of the individual human being—one's ultimate and decisive role in what one will do, be it right or wrong. Another path is the secular, neo-Aristotelian view in terms of which while human beings are rationally classifiable as such, one of their essential attributes is that they can and usually choose to be unique. So, in contrast to Marx's claim that "the human essence is the true collectivity of man,"[16] the classical individualist holds that "the human essence includes the true individuality of every human being."

In the radical individualist tradition a major libertarian element is the subjectivity of values. Accordingly, free market economists have tended to reject all government regimentation of social affairs, seeing them as driven by subjective preferences that cannot be known to anyone other than those who hold them. Such a view has served to undermine all efforts to impose values on individuals.

The classical individualist position argues that values are objective but also quite often idiosyncratic and they require free choice to give them moral significance. This too prohibits government imposition of values but not for skeptical reasons. Also, it enables one to defend the political value of liberty as more than simply one of many subjective preferences.

As far as free markets are concerned, one main reason they function more successfully than statist alternatives is that in a free market individual aspirations, goals, preferences, values, and such have a major impact on what will be produced. This in turn results in a more prosperous society than one where such individual goals and so forth are trumped by various so-called public-interest considerations that, in fact, are no more than the interest of vocal groups of individuals overriding that of others. Even the famous calculation problem identified by Austrian economists makes more sense if individualism is true. The reason governments cannot allocate or price goods and services properly is that such resources are ultimately (albeit objectively) valuable for individuals, not collectives.[17]

The individualism that underpins much of libertarian political economy has vital implications for public policy. In the law, for example, the position of criminal culpability gains support from it. The rejection of collective guilt—or pride—in social theory also has its support. In environmental public policy it makes clear sense of the ubiquitous phenomena of the tragedy of the commons, suggesting that human beings must have an individual stake in caring for resources before those resources can be expected to be well cared for. Public officials, since they can only represent a very general public interest—to secure the rights of individuals—have no clear-cut guide to policies of resource preservation and conservation. Individualism also underlies the rejection of the precautionary principle favored by environmentalists, whereby the mere possibility of future problems can be invoked to justify violating individual rights.[18]

Libertarianism is seen by most to rest on some version of individualism, although there are exceptions. Some believe that the betterment of society as a whole is what requires an individualist social and legal policy, even though there is nothing ultimately true about individualism. If, however, it is treated in public policy as if it were true, the results will be advantageous to the entire community. (Karl Marx held a view akin to this, claiming that for at least a stage of humanity's development—namely, capitalism—the illusion of individualism was very useful since it inspired a great deal of productivity.)

Still, it is difficult to see how libertarians can avoid being also individualists. This is especially true of those who stress the need for the protection of basic human rights in the Lockean individualist position.

Some Policy Implications

Libertarianism is, after all, a proposal to practice politics in a certain way, guided by a set of principles, yet it is not a rigid, deductive system of implied public policies. No functionally effective theory can be that, since the future is not fully disclosed to us and we need a system that provides flexibility. Constitutional law is based, roughly, on this insight: certain fundamental principles are accepted and supposed to remain stable and lasting, but the application of them can be novel and unpredictable. The basic principles are taken to be stable and lasting because they pertain to human community as such, meaning that they rest on certain known features of human nature and its requirements within society. It's akin somewhat to medicine, where medical students learn the general principles of human health but when they go into the field and apply these, much diversity and novelty can be expected.

At this point I wish to present just a few more specific libertarian ideas about political life. These are still rather general ideas, as they must be within the context of a discussion of political philosophy and theory. Also, they are not presented in some order of priority. Yet they will point to more particular issues than can be discussed when fundamental principles are the focus.

Government Regulations

Libertarianism rejects the justice of government regulations of business or any other profession or private activity—gambling, prostitution, drug use, and commerce—on the grounds that unless a person is violating another's rights (or is demonstrably threatening to do so), no one is justified in interfering with what that person is doing. Just as in the American legal system no one may interfere with any citizen speaking his or her mind, worshiping, or publishing written works, so in a free society no one, including the government, is justified in such interference. Such interference is best described by the legal term "prior restraint"—that is, imposing burdens or restrictions on the conduct of someone who has not been convicted of having violated or threatening the violation of someone's rights. It is only rights-violating conduct—involving one person or persons taking over the sovereignty of another—that justifies restraining a person, and the rights involved would have to be negative, not positive, rights, since the latter are actually impositions of servitude on persons. But let us spend a moment on the issue of negative versus positive rights, a subject to which I will be turning next.

Libertarianism—or those versions of the position that see the function of a legal order as the protection of individual rights—construes citizens as sovereign agents, whose self-governance or self-direction while living in communities is in need of respect and protection. Negative rights are the rights that prohibit uninvited intrusions or interference by some on others. An invited intrusion would be that performed by a surgeon or dentist; an uninvited intrusion would be that of a mugger or similar aggressor, as well as that of an official who has not obtained the consent of the citizens in whose life he or she is intruding. Negative rights are, then, borders that spell out one's sphere of jurisdiction or authority, and what belongs within one's jurisdiction includes one's life and the results of one's productive activities or freely acquired assets.

Someone's alleged positive right to health care or to the education of his or her children could only be secured if those who provide health care or education were required to provide it whether they have consented to doing so—or, alternatively, some would be required to perform productive labor the payment for which would be confiscated from them so as to pay the health or education providers. All of this is, as the late Robert Nozick observed, "on a par with forced labor," and so unjustified.[19] The claim that one has positive rights rests, mainly, on the belief that one comes into the world with obligations to other persons (not one's parents, who are due certain benefits for taking on the task of bringing one up). This is well put by August Comte, the father of sociology:

> Everything we have belongs then to Humanity . . . Positivism never admits anything but duties, of all to all. For its social point of view cannot tolerate the notion of *right*, constantly based on individualism. We are born loaded with obligations of every kind, to our predecessors, to our successors, to our contemporaries. Later they only grow or accumulate before

we can return any service. On what human foundation then could rest the idea of right, which in reason should imply some previous efficiency? Whatever may be our efforts, the longest life well employed will never enable us to pay back but an imperceptible part of what we have received. And yet it would only be after a complete return that we should be justly authorized to require reciprocity for the new services. All human rights then are as absurd as they are immoral.[20]

The idea is that since we benefit from what others have done over the centuries, we now owe something to the rest of humanity in return for these benefits. But this is to assume that we have agreed to receive the benefits on the terms that require us to pay up in this way. Moreover, it assumes that there are certain select persons, officials of the government, who are authorized to extract that payment. None of this is true. We often gain benefits from others—nice looking or smelling people we walk by, the works of art others have produced, architectural wonders they have created—without its being true that we owe them anything for this. (It is a fair assumption that those who freely produced and created all of this are well rewarded for what they did in a variety of ways, not the least of which is the joy of the process itself.)

So, the attempt to justify government regulation of people's peaceful conduct on the grounds that they owe everyone something—the basis of positive rights—fails. There are other reasons some invoke to support such regulation but those do not hold up either.[21]

Entitlements via Positive Rights

One of the most powerful ideas opposed to the free society is a notion political philosophers call *positive rights*, which is arguably another all-too-successful linguistic legerdemain, like that which overtook the venerable concept of "liberalism." "Liberalism" once specified a political philosophy favorable toward individual rights and (negative) freedom. Now, in today's lingo, it means nearly the opposite: an ideology prescribing the systematic violation of liberty for the sake of redistributing wealth and otherwise engineering society. (To be sure, the new liberalism includes a subclause stipulating that people may at least enjoy the sexual, pro-choice, and other noneconomic freedoms distinctive to one's chosen "lifestyle." But even these allowances are more and more falling victim to the logic of this liberalism's command-and-control statism—as when liberals and conservatives team up to urge censorship of sexually explicit fiction.) Just as the new "liberalism" is fake liberalism, so the new "positive rights" are fake rights. In each case, the heart of a valid principle has been gutted.

Natural rights—or, as they have been un-euphoniously dubbed, "negative rights"—pertain to freedom from the uninvited interventions of others. Respect for negative rights requires merely that we abstain from pushing each other around. Positive rights, by contrast, require the opposite. Fealty to positive rights requires that we be provided with goods or services at the expense of other persons, which can only be accomplished by systematical coercion. This idea is also known as the "doctrine of entitlements." That is to say, some people are said to be entitled to that which was earned or will be or could be earned by other people.

"Positive rights" trump freedom.[22] According to the doctrine of positive rights, human beings by nature owe, as a matter *of enforceable obligation,* part or even all of their lives to other persons. Generosity and charity thus cannot be left to individual conscience.

If people have basic positive rights, no one is justified in refusing service to others; one may be conscripted to do so regardless of one's own choices and goals. (The class of procedural positive rights—such as the right to vote, to receive a fair trial—relates to the government's obligations to citizens *once citizens have chosen to establish or institute a government or similar legal agency for purposes of securing their basic rights.* Thus several critiques of the libertarian idea that basic individual human rights are all negative—are misguided.[23] They argue, essentially, that negative rights come to nothing without the positive right to have them protected which they then dub as more fundamental than the negative rights that are to be protected. What they miss is that such positive rights, like all bona fide positive rights, are derived from the prior exercise of one's [not yet protected] negative right to establish a legal order.)

If positive rights are valid, then "negative rights" cannot be, for the two are mutually contradictory. So the question is: which of these two concepts is the more plausible, when we consider how the issue of rights arise to begin with, in the context of human nature and the requirements of survival and flourishing in a human community?

The rights Locke identified—following several centuries of political and legal thinking by theorists who had begun to identify them more or less precisely—are "negative" insofar as they require only that human beings *abstain or refrain from forcibly intruding on one another*. Their existence means that no one ought to enslave another, coerce another, deprive another of property, and that each of us may properly resist such conduct when others engage in it. Ordinary criminal law implicitly rests on such a theory of individual rights. On a commonsense basis, murder, assault, kidnapping, robbery, burglary, trespassing, and the like are all easily understood as violations of negative rights.

In the Lockean tradition, a conflict of (justified, true) rights cannot exist. There may be disputes about boundary lines, the exact historical record determining the propriety of a rights claim, and similar practical detail. But once the facts of the matter are unambiguously established, so is the specific right of the matter. The justice of that specific claim (to a parcel of land, say) is grounded in more basic, universal rights (to life and freedom), in turn justified by a correct understanding of human nature and what that implies about how we ought to live and organize ourselves in communities.

That an understanding of human nature is even possible is, among some philosophers anyway, a controversial issue. Yet skepticism here, as in other cases, stems from an unrealistic conception of what it takes to know something, to the effect that we must know everything perfectly before we can know anything at all. But if knowing something means to have the clearest, most self-consistent, most reality-grounded and most complete conceptualization possible to date (if not for all time) of what it is we supposedly know, sweeping skepticism is unjustified. We need simply admit that we will if necessary amend our knowledge if later observation and thinking warrants it, and go with what we know now. What we know now is that human beings, uniquely among the animal kingdom, survive by means of their reason (which is simultaneously a faculty of choice and hence of morality), that this moral and rational faculty does not function automatically, and that the social condition required to gain and retain the fruits of its unhindered exercise is *freedom*. If human beings are to survive and flourish in a social context, the human rights to life and liberty must be recognized and protected.

Those who sought to retain some elements of the political outlook which Locke's theory had overthrown—namely, the view that people are subjects of the head of state (do, in fact, belong to the state)—found a way to expropriate and exploit the concept of human rights to advance their reactionary position, just as they expropriated and exploited the concept of liberalism.

So much had the concept of human individual rights been perverted at its root that it came to mean not *liberty from* others but *service from* others. Who needs the right to pursue happiness when one has the right to be *made* happy (even if the thus-extracted "happiness" should render the indentured providers of it miserable).

This was a view of rights that wiped the fact of human moral agency right out of existence. Positive rights, so called, are thus nothing more than mislabeled preferences or values that people want the government to satisfy or attain for them—of course, by force.[24] They are grounded in nothing that pertains to the fundamental requirements of human nature and human survival. The theorizers of such rights in fact go out of their way to ignore such requirements. Yes, people need bread, as stipulated. But they do not live by bread alone. They are not ants, that can survive on whatever crumbs fate happens to strew in their path. They need the freedom to make the bread and trade the bread.

Also, they need consistent and objective governance. But when the conceptual perversion known as positive rights becomes the guiding principle of a polity, the state cannot govern by anything like the consistent standards that emerge from the theory of negative rights. The alleged positive rights of the citizenry must clash constantly. To the extent one is conscripted to serve another, one can no longer serve one's own purposes—nor, indeed, even the purposes of many others, given the scarcity of the time and skills to which others are supposedly naturally entitled. There is no principle implicit in the doctrine of positive rights which could resolve the conflicts. But positive rights conflict most of all with our basic negative rights to life, liberty, and property.

Guided by such a doctrine, governments cannot merely protect our rights. They must positively pit some rights against other rights. Instead of simply "securing these rights," they must scrounge for some additional standard by which to tell which and whose rights should get protection. Since no such intelligible standard is available, the situation collapses into one of rule not by objective law but by subjective men— men who will decide which rights need protection and which do not, on a shifting "case-by-case basis." Perhaps the ascendant pressure group of the moment will carry the day, or perhaps the latest opinion polls. In practice, the working (Hobbesian?) principle is: "You have a right to whatever you can get away with," the same consideration governing any plain criminal.

The theories defending positive rights are just as incoherent as the practice of them must be. Positive rights have even been defended on the grounds that negative rights—of the very poor, for example—entail these positive ones.[25] Others argue that all rights are in fact positive insofar as they are all meaningless unless they are actively protected, and that the right to the protection of one's right to freedom is a positive right, not a negative one.[26]

Both views suffer fatal flaws. The first generalizes into a principle of law of an understandable but regrettable response to what amounts to a rare moral emergency case—one that becomes more and more rare the longer a society is free and so able to build its prosperity. In some rare cases, an innocent person might indeed be totally helpless and have no choice but to obtain resources by stealing them. Perhaps only filching that piece of fruit will stave off immediate starvation. But extraordinary circumstances cannot generate laws granting a permanent right to steal, not when stealing itself *means* taking by force what by right belongs to others. There is no need for a society to send the occasional Jean Valjean to prison for twenty years; he might well be forgiven the transgression. On the other hand, if the general concern for the plight of such individuals is genuine, there is no reason private charity cannot suffice to meet the need, either. Moreover, for the members of a society to engage in theft as a regular way of life can only undermine the production of wealth that everyone's survival depends upon, including that of the poorest.

Others believe that we already have positive rights to the services of the state and, thus, to the earnings of taxpayers who must pay for these services. But they fail to show that any such right to protection provision can exist *unless* there already exists the more fundamental—and "negative"—right to liberty. To gain protection for something presupposes that one has the right to act for that purpose, including the right to voluntarily combine with others for the purpose of delegating authority, forming the government, and gaining the protection.

The services of government are something people must choose to obtain, by their consent to be governed. They do not have a natural right to them prior to having freely established that institution. Indeed, for this reason the institution of taxation, which fit well those regimes that treat people as subjects who live by permission or the ruling elite or monarch, is anathema to the free society wherein even the funding of the legal order must be secured voluntarily.[27]

A more recent version of the positive rights case for wealth redistribution is the capabilities approach, introduced by Amartya Sen[28] and defended also by Martha Nussbaum.[29] Just as with positive freedom, the right to freedom becomes *the right to be provided by others* with various goods and services, so with the capabilities approach the burden is placed on those who have goods and services—mostly funds that can be subjected to confiscatory taxation—so as to facilitate the development of those lacking them. The idea is defended on grounds, basically, of *need*—or, to use Nussbaum's terms, a "comprehensive concern with flourishing across all areas of life" which for her, not negligibly, also "is a better way of promoting choice than is the liberal's narrower concern with spontaneity alone, which sometimes tolerates situations in which individuals are in other ways cut off from the fully human use of their faculties."[30]

So, in order to enhance flourishing, including significant choice, Nussbaum and others seem to be willing to grant some people—the government—the power to compel other people to provide for those in need to at least whatever will secure for them the materials that satisfies such "comprehensive concern." The need, of course, does not arise because others have done anything to the needy, thus their enforceable obligation to alleviate it is dubious. At most others ought to extend help as a matter of their generosity.[31]

In Nussbaum and others, however, notice the assumption that since "something ought to be done," then "government ought to do it." Unless one assumes there is some semantic equivalence or direct implication between these two claims, a linking premise is needed. That this fallacious move places others into the position of subservience—even servitude—to those in such need appears to Nussbaum to be unproblematic. In a sense Nussbaum & Co. generalize globally the rationale offered for Good Samaritan laws, even though the latter pertain to emergencies (such as an injured party in need of medical attention after a car crash) and, in any case, are subject to the criticism that no one is to be put in anyone else's service against his or her will.[32]

The bottom line is that in all these cases it is alleged that human beings are entitled to provisions from unwilling others who have them and government officials are very much in the business of securing such entitlements. (Sen's works routinely use titles that include the concept of "freedom" but in the ambiguous sense whereby both negative and positive freedoms [!] are at issue for him and those who sympathize with his capabilities approach.)

This approach is natural to socialists who see human beings as essentially species beings. For nonsocialists, however, the defense of positive rights and the capabilities approach may be linked to the American idea—from the Declaration of Independence—that "governments are instituted" so as "to secure . . . rights." Although the rights to be secured were negative ones—to life, liberty, and the pursuit of happiness, among others—it makes sense for those who see government in the role of enabling people rather than protecting their sovereignty to introduce the idea of positive rights. These would then still require being secured by the government, although now by means of a vastly expanded administration involving wealth redistribution as a central function. The balancing between securing negative and positive rights would naturally become a central element of the political processes, issuing in repeated class-warfare-type political activism.

Because it is itself arbitrary and incoherent, the doctrine of positive rights leaves government free to be arbitrary and incoherent. As long as some people are getting resources that were earned by somebody else, that's all that counts. One day it's aiding AIDS research that tops the to-do list; the next it's fostering the arts by splurging on PBS; the next it's curing everyone of smoking and plundering the tobacco companies. No principles, no logic, no standards of restraint tell us from day to day what one will be free to do and what one will be prohibited from doing; there is no surefire way to know. As under fascism, whatever the leaders say, goes, so long as they continue to genuflect mechanically before the altar of democracy.

If we are to reverse course, and achieve a more consistently free society, we must tear up the counterfeit standard of rights and restore a gold standard—the standard that enables us to actually pursue, and achieve, life, and happiness.

Against Mandated Affirmative Action

Over the last few years the United States has required all government agencies at the federal and state levels—including firms doing business with the state and schools that are state administered—to practice affirmative action. Some claim that the phrase itself refers to a uniquely legal or public policy. It is, they claim, a term of art for this unique practice, not matched by anything apart from what government does.

Actually, the practice itself has always existed and only recently has been dubbed "affirmative action." It amounts to people's making an energetic, vigilant effort to benefit, in trade or other activities—including admission to schools, promotion to higher ranks in fire or police departments—some special group deemed to be disadvantaged. As such affirmative action is a rather familiar practice in life, albeit not so designated until recent times.

When one hires people or goes to a shop owned or operated by someone from an actually or apparently disadvantaged group—blacks, Hispanics, Italian, Hungarian, or Polish Americans—one is often embarking upon what is the desired behavior sought via affirmative action. Similarly, when one selects a restaurant because one believes those who own or are employed there need some extra support so as to gain a leg up in the business, one is engaging in affirmative action. The buying of works of art just to encourage artists or patronizing some store in the hope that those who run it will remain in business—even though at the moment one has no particular wish for its services or goods—counts as affirmative action as well.

Consumers and producers have for centuries embarked upon such practices. Some famous black Americans acknowledge this, as did the late Carl Rowan, a black journalist, when he told a group of students on C-Span that his "employer practiced affirmative action" when he got his first job as a reporter from a white publisher. The latter apparently decided to give Mr. Rowan a chance because he was black and he wanted blacks to gain access to journalism. This decision also paid off for the employer, given Mr. Rowan's excellent performance on the job.

The type of official affirmative action that's at issue in contemporary debate—for example, in connection with Proposition 209, the California referendum that went into effect a while ago, banning all preferential hiring by state agencies, whatever the motivation—has to do with government orders to select students or contractors on the basis of racial or sexual criteria not relevant for the purpose at hand. It is the government that selects the (groups of) people who are to be proper candidates for affirmative action, usually based on certain sociological and historical facts pertaining to the disadvantage many of the race or sex in question have suffered in the past and the assumed advantage accrued from such disadvantage to the dominant groups, usually Caucasians. By this means the matter of deciding who is to be the beneficiary of affirmative action and whether the practice is a good idea is taken out of the hands of those who have to carry out the policy.

Thus often those required to act affirmatively cannot claim credit for their occasional good judgment in adopting the practice since they carry it out under the threat of punishment. Of course, some might well have done the right thing anyway, just as some volunteer for service in a war even when conscription is in force. But for others, who act because the practice is mandated by law, any credit for the deed is voided by the bureaucrats, except in so far as having a minor say through the democratic representative process is concerned. Beyond this minimal genuine affirmative action expressed during the vote for a policy or person, many of those implementing affirmative action policies carry on as ordered, leaving it indeterminate as to whether they followed their conscience or merely complied.

When it comes to government's following affirmative action policies, another distinction needs to be kept in mind. A government which is confined to its proper scope of authority is under the fiduciary duty to serve well all those under its jurisdiction. That is the spirit underlying the Fourteenth Amendment to the Constitution—no citizen's due process (i.e., what the citizen is owed) is to be neglected by the government. We ought all to be treated equally well under the law, no one is special. That is what citizenship implies.

When governments engage in affirmative action, this principle is violated.[33] Government conducted affirmative action is procedurally unjust. Governments must relate to people as citizens, period, not as some special group in whom a special interest is taken. That is the only way government can be just—it is why justice is depicted as blind.

Some will argue that sometimes government must provide protection to special groups when their members are the target of injustice. Blacks, therefore, may receive special treatment, as per affirmative action policies, because they are targets of unjust discrimination, something that affirmative action would redress.

However, injustice is never a matter of how groups, but only of how their members, are being treated. Any redress must, therefore, be a matter of rectifying or punishing those who committed the injustice, not members of groups whose other members have been unjust to some persons. Affirmative action, therefore, administers collective punishment, something that is anathema to a system of justice that must respect and protect individual rights.

Let us return to private affirmative action. Even there it would be valid only in emergency, rare cases, such as those having to do with new arrivals in a country or, more generally, with people who may need a temporary break, as it were. A private company may elect to do this but is always open to criticism if the policy persists, discriminates unjustly, and undermines good business. Publicly held corporations, furthermore, could practice affirmative action only when those who own its stock have instructed management to do so. Since affirmative action, rightly understood, can only have a valid point when the details of a situation are well known—it must, in other words, amount to local policy contingent on special knowledge and circumstances—most publicly held companies would have little justification to practice it. (An exception might be if there is some disaster nearby and the company decides temporarily to lend a hand to its casualties.)

Government-conducted and dictated affirmative action is not only unjust but can become the source of serious resentment to anyone, be they racists or not. The following might help make this clear.

If one who is white were to call a black person a "nigger," that, however insulting it is, does not justify being beaten up for it. No one should be assaulted for being insulting, period, and that goes for whatever they say.

Now, in the same vein, people's sovereignty—their freedom, for example, to associate only with those who are willing—should not be usurped by government, even if their judgments and conduct leaves much to be desired. I may choose rotten pals, an unsuitable mate, or the wrong employee, but what I do must remain my choice, not that of others who impose their judgment against my will. (Of course, if I announce that my offer of a service or good is available to all potential purchasers, it can be legally actionable if I then impose an unannounced standard of selection after the fact. By the standard of the "reasonable person," it is to be expected that without full disclosure of special criteria, none will be applied.)

In any case, freedom to associate with those who are willing is a hallmark of a free society. This means freedom of association across the board, even in cases where such association is misguided by racial prejudice and where those affected forgo serious benefits as a result, ones they would enjoy were those with the prejudice acting more rationally, decently. The reason is that in associating with others—except where contracts specify otherwise or where one would violate another's basic and derivative rights—one is making a decision as to how one will live one's own life, be this judgment good or bad. To make a person devote his or her life—or any portion of it—to a purpose he or she rejects amounts to subjecting the person to involuntary servitude. No free society can tolerate this, even for purposes that can be quite admirable.

Law professor Richard Epstein[34] of the University of Chicago has argued the radical but sound thesis that even the bulk of civil rights legislation of the 1960s cannot be considered of real help to blacks and women in our society. Epstein agrees that such legislation is in violation of a fundamental principle of free societies, namely, freedom of association. Civil rights laws violate the right to freedom of association by forcing people to hire and promote folks they may not want to. By this means the spirit, if not the letter, of a vital and sound principle of the American constitutional system is assaulted. Whatever gains may have been reaped through such legal action are marred severely because of this fundamental flaw that is embodied in securing them. Indeed, all civil rights legislation is wrong that goes beyond striking down racist and sexist policies by government, ones that violate the provision of the Fourteenth Amendment prohibiting "the den[ial] to any person . . . equal protection of the laws"—so that cops and judges and government in general may not deliver services differentially to the citizens they serve.

Mandated affirmative action programs are also an insult to the people who are intended to be helped by it. Certainly blacks and women have suffered in the past from injustices, as have other groups throughout human history. To think that it is now necessary and proper to "even the scales" is wrong from several perspectives, not the least of which is that because the really guilty parties are mostly dead, one can punish only innocent people. This mirrors the practice in Ghana where a young virgin from a family is given to a priest so as to atone for the sins of some elder of that family. It is the height of injustice to punish the innocent just because the guilty are no longer around.

Accordingly, when citizens are restricted regarding who they hire or do business with, their own judgment is superceded by others and they are placed into servitude to others by such a policy. Among other things, this serves to obscure their own wrongdoing. It, furthermore, can seriously obstruct their own appreciation of the wrong they do. Indeed, policies such as mandated affirmative action encourage prejudice to linger, even if underground. For what folks will focus upon is not their own prejudicial conduct, which they might have been prompted to reflect upon by being treated as free, sovereign citizens who are in charge of their own lives, and had they been addressed as capable of changing their own free will of how they behave. Instead, they will focus upon the fact that their sovereignty has been denied, their freedom taken away, and in that regard they have a just complaint.

Affirmative action also gives the racists among us a rationalization for racism, only now their animosity toward a minority has some semblance of justification: if women and blacks support mandated affirmative action, is there not really something wrong with women and blacks? After all, they give backing to tyrannical policies of government.

It is also worth considering that mandated affirmative action may not really help those blacks and women who can use the help. Instead it is the middle-class blacks who appear to get from this government mandate a boost in their economic or professional lot. The very people who ought to continue to make it on their own and have every chance to do so appear to get the extra, unfair advantage. Those in genuinely bad straits often are not even touched by this facade of assistance.

But while arguably nothing much of substance gets done for most blacks by affirmative action, the policy does every-thing to boost the self-image of racist Americans. For now they can submerge their racism within a legitimate rage. They can now hate the government for imposing on people plainly unfair, even racist, policies.

What irony! Supporters justify this program on grounds that it supposedly creates a level playing field, one that is needed af-ter many decades of injustice inflicted upon those who are the subject of mandated affirmative action. In fact it appears instead to help exactly those who seem to have no desire for fairness and good sense about matters of gender and racial justice. These very people against whose mentality the programs were sup-posedly enacted now finally gain public sympathy in its wake. If one were a racist, this would be most welcome.

Another aspect of this policy is that it treats the minorities intended to be benefited as if they were inept at recovering from the damage that past injustice has inflicted upon them. Are blacks and women unable to rise from the ruins of their families? Jews, Hungarians, Poles, and millions of others throughout history had to recover without the benefit of the U.S. Congress, without allegedly remedial public policy in the way of mandated affirmative action. Arguably, this approach is only going to hamper the recovery itself, by instilling in folks the conviction that they are, after all, not quite up to han-dling problems the way others can. (Jim Sleeper makes this point in his *Liberal Racism*.)[35]

In the social realm it seems progress has been forthcom-ing, but it is obscured by all the hope invested in government remedies. These days, for example, being racist is not accept-able in the deep South. A while back I heard a hospital worker in Opelika, Alabama, make a racist remark about a black colleague. When I rebuked him for it—he made the racist comment to me—he said "I am sorry, I am a racist, but I cannot help it." His response reflected not self-righteousness but a desperate effort to seek some kind of excuse. This presupposes that the man knew very well that his racism is not something acceptable in a decent human being. Yet, I'll bet that if this guy were to lose a promotion to an African American because of mandated affirmative action, he would feel comfortable about hating them, under the guise of hating big government. How convenient, not having to live squarely with your vile, irrational feelings, having the government help you to disguise them as anger at oppression.

If any group has very good reason for opposing affirmative action mandates by the government, it is American blacks. It is, as Shelby Steele noted on the *PBS News Hour*, a way white liberals can feel good about themselves without actually having to do much of substance.

Against the War on Drugs, and for Tolerance

In an important essay in the now discontinued publication *Heterodoxy* ["Just Say Yes!" September 1996], Peter Collier dismisses the libertarian view on drug abuse by saying that its "strong appeal . . . is that it plays well with the American notion of rugged individualism and don't tread on me." After this dismissive, anti-intellectual characterization of the position's "appeal" (never mind the merits of the arguments behind it), Collier goes on to say that "its defect is that it nowhere acknowledges the enormous destructive power of psychoactive substances and their ability to cause the disintegration of individual personalities, families and communities, and the fact that it is based on the questionable assumption that individuals will act less anti-socially when drugs are legal and guilt free than they do now when they are illegal and stigmatized."

As a libertarian who has often advocated drug legalization, I know that Mr. Collier has got it wrong.[36] Most libertarians fully acknowledge all of what Mr. Collier claims they do not. Most of them do not predict with any measure of certainty that people "will act less anti-socially when drugs are legal," etc. What they claim is that people ought to and will be able to act less antisocially and will no longer act criminally as drug users, in light of the decriminalization of drug abuse.

Most of all, libertarians claim that it is morally wrong and bad public policy to punish people who violate no one's rights and who already punish themselves by abusing drugs. They argue that the mere fact that some vices are far more tempting, far more difficult to resist, than others does not justify the paternalistic actions of the state against those who lack the strength of will and character to resist. They defend legalization on the grounds of principles such as the right to one's life, one's liberty of conviction and action, and the right to one's private property, all of which are relentlessly abrogated by the drug war that Mr. Collier's statist approach to the problem supports. They add that allowing the state to intrude upon innocent citizens for this reason more or less opens the door for it to intrude for any other—as William Pitt the Younger noted, "Necessity is the plea for every infringement of human freedom. It is the argument of tyrants; it is the creed of slaves" (speech on the India Bill, November 1783).

Libertarians—albeit summoning somewhat different arguments for their conclusion (as it is to be expected from a diverse *and* individualist lot)—not only find the drug war, as well as all the drug, alcohol, and related prohibitions, be it in America or anywhere around the world, not only a sustained, unremitting violation of individual rights but a demoralizing approach to helping people who find it very tough to deal with drugs. They consider it a social calamity when governments posture as Florence Nightingales, thereby displacing the much more promising avenue of rescue via the work potentially available from local communities—families, friends, professional associations, religious groups, etc., all of which are better positioned to address drug-related problems than is any level of government.

Conclusion

Libertarianism rests on numerous ideas drawn from various disciplines, and none of those could be fully explored here. The thrust of the position should by now be plain enough: Individuals are responsible to live their lives properly and ethically, and this requires that they be able to choose how to act. Further, within their communities they require a sphere of personal authority or jurisdiction, which is best secured via a well-protected set of basic rights, including the right to private property. Individuals have the right to pursue their happiness by forming special communities, provided all members choose to be part of them and everyone enjoys what the economists so quaintly call "the exit option." It is the role in their general communities—in the polity—of the legal order or government to secure their rights, and for this the people entrusted with that role must strictly abide by due process, which is to say, eschew the violation of rights as they secure rights themselves.[37]

Some have charged that libertarianism is utopian and for that reason alone a bad idea. Libertarianism is, of course, the consistent, uncompromising development of certain notions we are all familiar with—for example, the barring of physical force from human relations, the requirement that even as we retaliate against or fend off coercive physical force, we need to act with restraint, or that one of the differences between human and other living beings is that the former can, if they act with discipline and perseverance, exclude brute force from their community lives (that is, they can be *civilized*).

As such, libertarianism is demanding, because it has no tolerance for anyone's, including government's, coercive meddling for any purposes whatever. Government—which is to say, certain other people—is not to be our daddy, nanny, or uncle; it is to be our civilized bodyguard.

The reasoning behind these ideas is not simple, but it includes one crucial fact that immediately refutes the claim that libertarianism is utopian. That is that human beings are in fact incapable of being forced to be morally good. It is up to them whether they will, or whether they will fail in that all-important task. We have free will, and we ought to excel at being human individuals, but there is no formula by which that goal can be guaranteed. Indeed, one reason government must be limited is that it wields a very dangerous weapon, namely, physical force, a weapon that may only be used by people who know their limits clearly and well; otherwise those in government, who are just like us, become despotic, tyrannical.

Utopia, in contrast, is a form of society wherein morality is guaranteed, where everyone is going to do what is right and be happy and fulfilled. Shangri-La is a good example, as were Sir Thomas More's *Utopia* and Karl Marx's communism. In those proposed societies the objective is to secure for everyone, by means of political organization and action, perfect fulfillment. (That is why Marx could envision the withering away of government itself, since once utopia has been reached there will be no need for law enforcement—all of us will be law abiding, automatically.)

It is clear from just this brief contrast between libertarianism and utopianism that the two are opposites. No, libertarianism is not dystopian—not, that is, based on the view that social life must turn out terribly. It is entirely noncommittal about how good people will turn out to be, with the one provision: when people are free and their rights are protected, the chances that they will be good and decent are better than if they can dump their mistakes on their fellows with impunity (as they can, for example, in the welfare state that we live in now).

There is no doubt, of course, that libertarianism is demanding. But all standards are demanding—they require of us to do our best, according to certain terms. However, libertarianism recognizes that doing our realistic best requires freedom and also runs the risk that we will fail. So there can be no guarantees as far as the libertarian is concerned when it comes to how good people will be once they are free. They are, however, more likely to be better than they are when they are oppressed, regimented, and ordered about in their daily lives.

The bulk of the challenges of human life, in all realms, should be tackled without aid of coercive force, something that critics of libertarianism seem to reject. Once the legal order secures everyone's rights—or does as well as possible at this task—it needs to withdraw and leave free men and women to meet the nonpolitical challenges they face. That is the crux of libertarianism.[38]

Notes

1. There are different routes to libertarian political conclusions, and in this discussion I will be sketching one within the normative natural law and rights tradition, not a consequentialist, utilitarian, or positivist one. It is my view that the widely championed consequentialist approach, which appears to reject principles in favor of expected utilities—so that, for example, a regime of liberty is just because it maximizes value—has serious problems, since the value of consequences cannot be assessed without principles as standards for evaluating them. There is also the non-consequentialist assumption in most versions of consequentialism that the results of policies can be correctly estimated before they occur. Yet that is just what the more principled approach to politics—and libertarianism in particular—contends. For more, see Tibor R. Machan, *The Passion for Liberty* (Lanham, Md.: Rowman & Littlefield, 2003), chap. 3, "Against Utilitarianism: Why Not Violate Rights If It Would Do Good?"

2. For a defense of this, see Tibor R. Machan, ed., *Individual Rights Reconsidered: Are the Truths of the U.S. Declaration of Independence Lasting?* (Stanford Calif.: Hoover Institution, 2001), especially Ronald Hamowy, chap. 1, "The Declaration of Independence." This, of course, is a mere historical fact, not any argument for the stance itself.

3. G. A. Cohen's complaint that disadvantaged workers are forced to work, therefore, is no argument against a capitalist, free market system. Life forces nearly everyone to work. See his "Are Disadvantaged Workers Who

Take Hazardous Jobs Forced to Take Hazardous Jobs?" in *Moral Rights in the Workplace*, ed. Gertrude Ezorsky, 61–80 (Albany: State University of New York Press, 1987). For a discussion of a libertarian view of labor, see Tibor R. Machan, "Rights and Myths at the Workplace," in *Moral Rights in the Workplace*, 45–50, and James E. Chesher, "Employment and Ethics," in *Commerce and Morality*, ed. Tibor R. Machan, 77–93 (Lanham, Md.: Rowman & Littlefield, 1988).

4. For more on this, see Tibor R. Machan, *Generosity: Virtue in Civil Society* (Washington, D.C.: Cato Institute, 1998), chap. 6, "Generosity *via* Government."

5. For a detailed discussion of this issue, see Tibor R. Machan, "Anarchism and Minarchism, A Rapprochement," *Journal des Economists et des Estudes Humaines* 14 (December 2002): 569–88. See also Aeon Skoble, *Freedom, Authority, and Social Order* (Chicago: Open Court, 2005).

6. Available at www.usdreams.com/LincolnW7.html.

7. Charles Taylor, *Philosophy and the Human Sciences* (Cambridge, U.K.: Cambridge University Press, 1985), 188. For more on this, see Tibor R. Machan, "Libertarian Justice," in *Social and Political Philosophy: Contemporary Perspectives*, ed. James P. Sterba, 93–114 (London, U.K.: Routledge, 2001). An important element of rights theory is identified in Douglas B. Rasmussen and Douglas J. Den Uyl, *Liberty and Nature* (Chicago, Ill: Open Court, 1990). The authors understand rights to be *meta-norms*, meaning these are principles of the societal *framework* within which action-guiding ethical or moral principles may be followed or neglected. A society with basic Lockean rights is one that secures for everyone the opportunity to be a moral agent.

8. See, for a libertarian interpretation of "general welfare," www.house .gov/science/taylor_4-9.html.

9. I have argued, in "America's Founding Principles and Multiculturalism," chapter 6 of my book *Classical Individualism* (London: Routledge, 1998), that in comparison to other political systems, the relatively libertarian polity of the United States accommodates the requirements of multiculturalism better than do others wherein conformity to common practices is stressed far more than is diversity and, especially, individuality.

10. Libertarians tend, in the main, to oppose wars of liberation or national building, not because it is wrong to help with such efforts abroad but a country's military already has a job, namely, to secure and defend the rights of the citizens there.

11. Available at www.adherents.com/.

12. Equality is, of course, a core value in libertarianism, only it is the equality of respecting the rights of individuals—all of them—rather than the equality of sharing benefits and burdens available in society. This latter type of equality, perhaps better dubbed "fairness," is supported from

various perspectives, but the crucial public policy implication of it concerns regimenting people's lives whenever benefits and burdens are not shared equally. That, as Robert Nozick demonstrated in his famous Wilt Chamberlain case, would require massive inequality of power and be not only intolerably coercive but self-defeating as well. See Robert Nozick, *Anarchy, State, and Utopia* (New York: Basic Books, 1974), 161–63.

13. A comparable approach is deployed by Martha Nussbaum, "Human Functioning and Social Justice: In Defense of Aristotelian Essentialism," *Political Theory* 20 (1992): 202–46, albeit with different substantive results for political theory—to wit, a robust welfare state and global wealth redistribution. Nussbaum, along with Amartya Sen, defends the view that human nature can be known from our historical encounters with human beings, but what our knowledge of it suggests is that social justice must involve a mainly egalitarian wealth-redistribution policy so as to enable everyone to flourish. The libertarian insistence on the vital importance of individual moral choice and responsibility is missing from her politics.

14. I draw on David L. Norton, *Personal Destinies, A Philosophy of Ethical Individualism* (Princeton, N.J.: Princeton University Press, 1976), and my own *Classical Individualism: The Supreme Importance of Each Human Being* (London: Routledge, 1998) for this distinction.

15. J. D. P. Bolton, *Glory, Jest and Riddle: A Study of the Growth of Individualism from Homer to Christianity* (New York: Barnes and Noble, 1973).

16. Karl Marx, "Critical Remarks on the Article: 'The King of Prussia and Social Reform,'" in *Selected Writings*, ed. David McClellan (Oxford, U.K.: Oxford University Press, 1977), 126.

17. For more on this, see Ludwig von Mises, *Economic Calculation in the Socialist Commonwealth* (Auburn, Ala.: Ludwig Von Mises Institute, 1990).

18. For more on this, see Tibor R. Machan, *Putting Humans First: Why We Are Nature's Favorite* (Lanham, Md.: Rowman & Littlefield, 2004).

19. Nozick, *Anarchy, State, and Utopia,* 169.

20. August Comte, *The Catechism of Positive Religion* (Clifton, N.J.: Augustus M. Kelley, 1973), 212–13.

21. See Tibor R. Machan and James E. Chesher, *A Primer on Business Ethics* (Lanham, Md.: Rowman & Littlefield, 2003), chap. 16–26; see also Tibor R. Machan, *Private Rights and Public Illusions* (New Brunswick, N.J.: Transaction Books, 1995) and Tibor R. Machan, "Government Regulation vs. the Free Society," *Business and Professional Ethics Journal* 22 (2003): 77–83.

22. Not, of course, in every sense of that term. "Freedom" can mean just what positive rights secure for someone, as made clear in the discussion in note 9. Consider, for example, the following: "No, life is always a struggle for freedom. Whenever I sign a cheque for some idiot company or other, I feel a little like a man in an electric chair or in a hospital bed, streaming with

wires and connections and linkages." James Wood, *The Book against God* (New York: Farrar, Straus and Giroux, 2003), where the first person protagonist consider himself to be free if he can escape the bonds of obligation he himself has incurred and that others, in turn, are made to assume.

23. In recent times the doctrine has been reshaped by such philosophers as Ronald Dworkin, James P. Sterba, Henry Shue, and legal scholars like Stephen Holmes and Cass R. Sunstein. Shue's *Basic Rights* (Princeton, N.J.: Princeton University Press, 1983) goes so far as to argue that no negative rights exist at all, since in any realistic sense rights are meaningless unless given protection, which is a positive service from others. But Shue forgets that the libertarian establishes secondary, derivative positive rights without contradicting himself, via compact and contract. Holmes and Sunstein, who echo Shue twenty-one years later, also fail to appreciate the idea that protecting rights via government and law requires consent. As the Declaration of Independence puts it so succinctly, governments derive "their just powers from the consent of the governed."

24. For a full exposition of the positive rights doctrine as developed by theorists of the political left, see Tom Campbell, *The Left and Rights* (London and Boston: Routledge, 1983).

25. See, Sterba, note 7 above.

26. See, e.g., Shue, note 23 above.

27. For a more detailed discussion of this issue, including viable alternatives to taxation, see Tibor R. Machan, "Dissolving the Problem of Public Goods: Financing Government without Coercive Measures," 28, in *The Libertarian Reader*, ed. T. R. Machan (Lanham, Md.: Rowman & Littlefield, 1982).

28. Amartya Sen, "Markets and Freedoms: Achievements and Limitations of the Market Mechanism in Promoting Individual Freedoms," *Oxford Economic Papers* 45 (1995): 519–41. See, on the recently launched capabilities approach project, the explanation provided at: www.fas.harvard.edu/~freedoms/capability_defined.html.

29. Nussbaum, "Human Functioning." A similar conception of human rights to welfare or empowerment is defended by Alan Gewirth, *Reason and Morality* (Chicago: University of Chicago Press, 1978). For libertarian critiques of Gewirth's political views, see Eric Mack, "Deontologism, Negative Causation, and the Duty to Rescue," and Douglas J. Den Uyl and Tibor R. Machan, "Gewirth and the Supportive State," in *Gewirth's Ethical Rationalism*, ed. Ed Regis, Jr. (Chicago: University of Chicago Press, 1984).

30. Nussbuam, "Human Functioning," 225–26. Another contemporary theorist who advances an argument along similar lines is Jürgen Habermas, *The Inclusion of the Other: Studies in Political Theory*, eds. Ciaran Cronin and Pablo De Greif (Cambridge, Mass.: MIT Press, 1998), whose conception of a just society based on discursive democracy involves various prerequisites

that will enable the citizenry to be able to take part in the discussion of public policy. Of course, the discussion then focuses on incidentals, since the important issue of whether such provisions must be made is already settled before the discussion gets under way. For more on this, see Tibor R. Machan, "Individualism and Political Dialogue," in *Classical Individualism* (London: Routledge, 1998), chap. 13.

31. See Machan, *Generosity, Virtue*.

32. One standard justification for Good Samarian laws is that they apply to professionals, such as doctors, who have gone on record offering their services to those in dire medical need, that the law merely spells out the occasion when that offer must be delivered. Still, even this rationale has problems, as shown in Mack, "Deontologism."

33. That is one reason the California law enacted by Proposition 209 makes good sense, though its substance should never have required a referendum.

34. Richard Epstein, *Forbidden Grounds* (Cambridge, Mass.: Harvard University Press, 1992).

35. Jim Sleeper, *Liberal Racism* (New York: Viking, 1997).

36. See, for example, Tibor R. Machan and Mark Thornton, "The Re-Legalization of Drugs," *Freeman* 41, no. 4 (April 1991): 153–55.

37. This is not the whole story or the whole problem with critics of the libertarian stance. In any case, those who wish to explore the various libertarian approaches to the problem of drug abuse—including the failed policies of the federal and local governments on this problem—can begin by checking the bibliography of (and reading) Mark Thornton's essay, "The Repeal of Prohibition," in *Liberty for the 21st Century*, eds. T. R. Machan and D. B. Rasmussen (Lanham, Md.: Rowman & Littlefield, 1995).

38. For a somewhat longer outline of libertarianism, see Tibor R. Machan, *The Liberty Option* (London: Imprint Academic, 2003). For a good selection of varied libertarian ideas, see Tibor R. Machan, ed., *The Libertarian Alternative* (Chicago: Nelson-Hall, 1974); Machan, *The Libertarian Reader;* and David Boaz, ed. *The Libertarian Reader* (New York: Free Press, 1997).

2

The Errors of Libertarianism

Craig Duncan

As a political philosophy, libertarianism has a certain seductive allure. Who among us, after all, enjoys paying taxes or likes having his or her actions constrained by laws? Our aversion to these things makes it tempting to think, like libertarians, that taxes and laws either should not exist or should exist only in forms radically reduced from their present levels. Despite its somewhat seductive allure at the abstract level, however, we have good reason to reject libertarianism. In arguing against it, I will make four major objections to it: the "Unanchored Property Objection," the "Inadequate Defense of Dignity Objection," the "Dilemma of Consent Objection," and the "Insufficiency of Charity Objection." To these objections I now turn.[1]

1. The Unanchored Property Objection

Interestingly, Professor Machan's libertarianism and my democratic liberalism (which I defend in chapter 4) share something in common at the level of foundations: they both purport to be grounded in respect for human beings' distinctive capacity for choice. Despite sharing a common foundation at the most abstract level, however, Machan and I differ very significantly in our concrete interpretations of the moral ideal of respect for the human capacity of choice. For instance, according to Machan this ideal entails that individuals have an absolute moral property right to all the money or goods they receive via market exchanges, whereas on my view the ideal instead entails that legal rights to property should be defined in a way that ensures all individuals have fair access to a life of dignity. Exploring this difference will reveal a large gap in the argument for libertarian property rights.

According to Machan, taxation is a form of theft (p. 26). This claim of Machan's has to be understood with care, however. As the law stands, you do not have legal title to all the pre-tax money that others pay to you in form of wages, salaries, sales, etc. You only have legal title to your after-tax earnings. Thus libertarians like Machan must concede there is no illegal crime of stealing involved with taxation. Instead, Machan must argue that taxation is the *moral equivalent* of stealing. Hence he must argue that people have a moral right to keep and control all their earnings—that is to say, a right that exists independently of any government-created laws or other conventions, much like the human rights not to be murdered, tortured, enslaved, and so on.

Several fatal problems beset this view of moral rights to property. An analogy will help make these flaws vivid. Suppose Annie is an antiques dealer who sells her wares from a small stall housed in a large building containing an antiques market, with many other dealers selling their wares at similar stalls. The building's owner, suppose, charges vendors a percentage of their sales intake—say, 20 percent—as payment for the opportunity to sell from one of the building's stalls. If Annie's earnings in sales for a given month were $2,400, then although that amount of money is in her possession, it is not hers, if by "hers" is meant legal ownership; $480 of those dollars in fact legally belong to the building's owner. The owner is not stealing her money when he demands this sum from her. Suppose that Annie recognizes this but goes on to protest that the antique mall owner's commission charge violates her moral right to keep all of her sales earnings. The obvious reply to Annie's charge is that but for the market owner's initiative and effort—in constructing the building and the stalls, in maintaining it, in securing it, in advertising its existence, and so on—Annie would not have had the opportunity to acquire any sales earnings in the first place. This makes it churlish at best and exploitative at worst for her to insist that she has a moral right to every penny of her sales.

Something similar is true of government taxes; after all, the existence of our economic opportunity is highly dependent on the government's activities of enforcing contracts, protecting legal property rights, keeping the peace, maintaining the national defense, printing currency, insuring bank deposits, preventing monopolies, fighting inflation, negotiating trade agreements, maintaining transportation infrastructure, and so on.[2] As in the case of Annie the antiques vendor, then, to insist that one has a moral right to all of one's income earnings is to ignore the efforts of one's fellow citizens who work in government or who as taxpayers contribute to the support of the government.[3] "Sure, without my fellow citizens' work I wouldn't have been able to earn the money I did," the libertarian seems to say, "but that doesn't mean I owe my fellow citizens anything for their work." The exploitative nature of this is obvious; this surely means that in fact one has no moral right to *all* of one's pre-tax earnings. A moral right to commit the moral wrong of exploiting one's fellow citizens would, after all, be a strange moral right indeed.[4]

Importantly, this skeptical conclusion certainly does not mean that taxation is always immune to moral criticism. There can be schemes of taxation that are tilted too heavily against low-income earners, or schemes that are tilted too heavily against high-income earners, so that the taxes levied are justifiably judged unfair. The guiding ideal in judging this question of fairness is one of *reciprocity:* there should be at least some rough balance between the benefits one gains and the burdens one shoulders in contributing to society. (For more details on this ideal of reciprocity, see my essay in chapter 4.) *This* potential sort of moral criticism of tax schemes, however, is off limits to libertarians like Machan, for according to him it is wrong for ideals of fairness to shape laws and public policy; laws and public policy must be confined purely to defending individuals' rights. (In the following section, I will in fact argue that individuals have rights to fair treatment, but in this section I will not pursue this line of thought.) Hence Machan's need to object (implausibly) to taxes on the grounds that they violate an absolute moral property right to all of one's pre-tax earnings, rather than on grounds of fairness.

There is another important objection to Machan's claim that one has a moral property right to every penny of one's pre-tax earnings. This is that Machan's claim does not follow from the foundation he provides for it. In fact Machan devotes scant attention to the task of justifying property rights—much less attention than this task warrants, given the importance of property rights to libertarianism. What argument there is apparently comes with the following sentence: "The right to private property, via property law in developed communities, secures for everyone a sphere of personal jurisdiction so it can be determined when one is acting within one's own sphere or intrudes on the spheres of others" (p. 13; cf. p. 38).

The problem is that legal property rights of the sort we already have in the United States—rights that legally allow for taxation—suffice to define adequately each individual's sphere of personal jurisdiction. One does not need rights to every penny of one's pre-tax earnings in order simply to define these spheres. How many of us, after all, currently have our lives blighted by uncertainty as to whether the actions we take with our possessions are legal or illegal?[5]

I presume Machan's actual thought is that maximal property rights are necessary to create a maximal sphere of personal jurisdiction—a maximal sphere of *liberty*, in a word. It is fallacious, however, to think that maximal property rights lead to maximal liberty, even when the liberty in question is negative liberty. To see this, consider that if, say, Susan owns a field, then although *she* has negative liberty to use the field, as a result of her ownership *other people* lack the negative liberty to use this field except by her permission; unauthorized users of it will find themselves on the wrong side of the law.[6] This can all be quite proper; I agree that there should indeed be some sort of legal property rights to personal belongings available to citizens. My point is just that libertarian property rights are not straightforwardly entailed by the value of negative liberty. This fact is easiest to appreciate if one imagines that the libertarians' wishes are granted and everything that can be privatized is, so that all roads are privately owned toll roads, all parks are privately owned admission-charging parks, all libraries are run like Blockbuster Video stores, and so on. In such a scenario, a poor person who could not afford road tolls, admission charges, and the like, might have no negative liberty to go anywhere whatsoever.

There is yet another well-known problem facing any account of a moral right to property, commonly known as the problem of "initial acquisition." Machan's proposed moral right to property is, after all, a right to keep whatever items come one's way through voluntary exchanges. But what are these voluntary exchanges? They are voluntary exchanges *of property*, of course. Thus the moral value of voluntary exchange presupposes the existence of property rights of some form; one cannot derive such rights from this moral value alone. Consider an example: I give you fifty dollars, say, in voluntary exchange for your jacket. In order for this to be a permissible exchange, I must already own the fifty dollars, and you must already own the jacket. Also, of course I acquired my fifty dollars and you acquired your jacket via earlier voluntary exchanges of things we previously owned, and so forth and so on back into time. But how did the whole process get going? There must have once been a point where some unowned

resource—a parcel of land, say—came to be owned by someone, in an act of initial acquisition. But how should this acquisition have happened ideally? Through some process of
"finders keepers," or something else? Machan does not say.

I conclude, then, that Machan has supplied no foundation
in which to anchor the incredibly strong moral rights to property that lie at the heart of his libertarianism.[7]

2. The Inadequate Defense of Dignity Objection

We have seen that both Machan's libertarianism and my democratic liberalism purport to be grounded in an ideal of respect for
the distinctive human capacity for choice—that is, an ideal of respect for the distinctive dignity of humans. We have already seen,
however, one important difference of interpretation regarding
this idea, a difference concerning property rights. In this section I
will examine another difference in interpretation, one concerning
the legitimate uses of force in defense of others' dignity.

According to libertarianism, force can be legitimately used
in only a few types of situations.[8] The kernel of truth in libertarianism's hostility to force is that there is indeed a strong
moral presumption against force, inasmuch as subjecting others to force bypasses their valuable capacity for choice. On
Machan's extreme interpretation of this truth, we can apparently override this presumption and permissibly use force
only in two cases: when the person subjected to force has himself or herself earlier authorized the use of force (by consenting to a legally binding contract, say) and when the person
himself or herself fails to respect another person's dignity by
intentionally using physical force to interfere with the other
person's choices, as is the case with murder, assault, and theft.
By contrast, my theory allows the use of force in additional
cases. This is so because a person can fail to respect another's
dignity in more ways than just the single way of intentionally
using physical force to interfere with the other's choices.

These other ways are possible because there is after all such a thing as *economic power* over others.[9] The power to hire a person (or not) is obviously a significant form of power. Additionally, being fired from one's job can be a serious disruption to one's life. A failure to be promoted as expected can also seriously disrupt one's plans. Thus people with the ability to hire, fire, and promote other people (or not) have a significant sort of power. This is inevitable, so long as firings and refusals to hire or promote people are possible, as they should be in some fashion. But as with political power (the abuse of which libertarians are so fond of noting) this private economic power can be abused: on a societal level, economic discrimination against minorities can be used to maintain a castelike system of social stratification; on an individual level, employees can (among other things) be threatened with job loss or lack of promotion unless they dispense sexual favors, perform unreasonably dangerous tasks, work an insane number of hours, or do other humiliating things they would never do but for their employer's power over them.

Fortunately, the state's power can be used to make these private forms of power more accountable, by (among other things) enabling some form of sexual harassment suits; enabling the formation of employee organizations (e.g., unions); and by passing anti-discrimination laws, health and safety laws, minimum-wage laws, and mandatory overtime-pay laws. The abuses of economic power listed above are abuses in virtue of being acts of exploitation, which we can define as taking unfair advantage of a person's vulnerabilities. More specifically, exploitative exchanges are not appropriately reciprocal; in them, one party is treated more as an instrument for another's private gain, rather than as a person in his or her own right. In this way the exploited party's dignity as a person is insulted. The same is true of unfair treatment generally—the recipient of unfair treatment is not treated as a person whose worth is equal to others. Unfairness is a threat to dignity.

In short, there are other serious sorts of threats to human dignity beyond the threat of intentional, forcible, physical interferences with other people's choices. If the importance of dignity grounds rights against *this* threat to one's dignity, as libertarians believe, then surely it also grounds rights against other threats to dignity. Such rights include a right to fair access to economic opportunity, a right to fair access to personal security (for one's body and property), a right to fair access to political influence, and a right to fair access to criminal justice (that is, a right to a fair trial).

We should now ask whether these rights are "positive rights," as Machan understands them. A simple answer of yes or no is not possible here; these "fairness rights" are like Machan's idea of positive rights in some respects, and unlike them in others. Fairness rights are like Machan's idea of positive rights in that their observance will require positive efforts from others, rather than merely the sort of forbearance shown in refraining from murder, assault, and theft. This is so because (as I say in chapter 4) like most other good things in life, fairness is not free of charge. Fairness does not spontaneously occur, like the beauty of a sunset. Fair access to political influence will require the funding of voting booths, ballot printing, tallying machines and workers to operate them; a right to fair trial will require the funding of highly trained judges, stenographers, and public defenders for indigent defendants, not to mention courthouses, law books, and the like. Fair access to economic opportunity will require some system of publicly funded education so that ignorance does not radically reduce the opportunities open to children of poor or negligent parents. Fair access to personal security will require some public protective system of police, prisons, and armed forces. The rather horrifying alternative of private protective associations (private, for-profit police forces, which one hires on one's behalf) would at best lead to a situation in which the wealthy have superb protection and the poor have meager protection or none at all—a security analogue of the current health care situation in the United States.[10]

Thus fairness rights are like Machan's idea of positive rights in that their observance costs something. However, they are unlike Machan's idea of positive rights in other regards. First, they are not a "right to be made happy," as Machan says (p. 24). Instead they are *access* rights. A right to a fair trial, for instance, does not guarantee you will be found innocent. A right to fair access to economic opportunity does not guarantee you will be happy; you must make yourself happy by working to make use of your opportunities. A right to a fair vote does not guarantee your favorite candidate will win— and so on. Second, fairness rights are not necessarily rights against everyone in the world. Instead they are first and foremost rights against the institutions that possess power over you; that is, they are rights to fair treatment at the hands of these institutions, and thus they are rights against all those participants who have the power to shape these institutions. For example, the right to fair access to economic opportunity is most fundamentally a right against your government, insofar as its laws create and sustain the economic system that prevails in your country. Inasmuch as our government is a democracy, moreover, the right to fair access to economic opportunity is a right against your fellow citizens, who have power to influence the government. Note, however, that correlative with this right there is also a duty. As an economic participant, we might say, you have a moral right that the economic system into which you were born ensure you fair access to economic opportunity, but as a citizen you have a moral duty to do your fair share of the work needed to support a fair economic system. Thus these are not rights to get anything for free.[11]

In short, Machan's objections that positive rights are rights to be made happy, or to get something for free, do not work against the fairness rights that I have defended. One other objection Machan makes is that positive rights conflict with negative rights. "If positive rights are valid," he says on page 23, "then 'negative rights' cannot be, for the two are mutually contradictory." This is mysterious. The rights to a fair trial, to fair access to economic opportunity, and so on, certainly do not stand in contradiction to one's negative rights against murder, assault, censorship, religious persecution, and so on. A state can define and protect all these rights simultaneously. To be sure, inasmuch as respecting positive rights requires economic contributions from many people, positive rights do conflict with one alleged negative right, namely, a property right to all of one's pre-tax earnings. As I have argued in section 1, however, it is implausible to suppose that this alleged negative right exists.

Finally, it is likely that Machan would make yet another objection, namely, that it is a mistake to see these rights (as I do) as fundamental, pre-legal rights. Instead, says Machan (p. 22), these rights, when they exist, are established contractually, by citizens consenting to a government. If by this he means that the rights to a fair trial, to an equal vote, etc., exist only in the case where citizens have created a government that legally recognizes these rights, then I disagree. Fairness rights exist whenever relations of power exist. Since government is a power-wielding institution, we can and should judge its laws by asking whether they respect citizens' fairness rights. The problem with Machan's alternative, consent-based view will be explored in the next section.

3. The Dilemma of Consent Objection

Machan places himself in a tradition dating back to John Locke by insisting that in order to be legitimate a government must obtain the consent—even if only the tacit consent—of all the citizens under its authority.[12] Unfortunately Machan's failure to provide much detail regarding the nature of tacit consent leaves his position open to several important objections. First, what counts as tacit consent to a government's authority? Does mere residence in a country suffice, as Locke believed?[13] If this is Machan's view, it is unconvincing. As the eighteenth-century philosopher David Hume pointed out in criticism of Locke, the burdens of exiting one's society and settling in a new one are high enough to make exit an intolerable or nonexistent option for most people. There is the cost of moving to and resettling in a foreign country, in addition to the burdens of adjusting to a new culture and possibly a new language.[14] One may have moral duties (e.g., caring for elderly parents) that tie one to a specific locale. Finally, and most decisively, one simply may not be able to find another country that will legally let one in. For the majority of people, then, remaining in the society of their birth is not a choice in any significant sense, and thus their residence cannot plausibly be construed as an act of tacit consent to society's authority.

Even if Machan were somehow able successfully to rebut this objection, it is not clear to me that a "residence = tacit consent" claim genuinely supports his position. For, of course, Machan wants to limit sharply government's authority, but an undemanding account of tacit consent threatens to legitimate all manner of activities that he regards as illegitimate. For example, the Swedish government, with its heavily regulated economy and its high levels of redistributive taxation, is antithetical in most ways to libertarianism. But if simply remaining in Sweden counts as tacitly consenting to the government there, then Machan must concede there is nothing illegitimate about Sweden's decidedly non-libertarian government.

Alternatively, Machan can opt for a more demanding version of tacit consent. There are problems, however, with this option. If residence does not suffice for tacit consent, there will surely be individuals living within a country's borders who do not consent to the government there. Maybe they want no government at all, or a more socialist government, a more libertarian government, a more religious government, or whatever. Will such individuals be permitted to stay in society but be exempt from its laws? This would destroy the rule of law. Instead, will such individuals be told to secede and convert what land they own into their own sovereign nation? This will not do either. A choice of "either consent or secede," like the choice of "consent or move abroad," is an empty one for most people; rejecting the unrealistic option of secession hardly suffices for tacit consent. Moreover, even when someone *is* willing to convert his land into a separate nation, it is foolish to permit this. Swiss cheese–style secession is undoubtedly a recipe for eventual societal breakdown and its attendant dangers.

Hence, making government's authority contingent on all of its citizens' consent runs into problems no matter how one understands consent. The best response to this dilemma is simply to concede that political society, owing to its territorial nature, is unlike other associations to which one might belong; one is simply born into it, rather than voluntarily deciding to join. It would be nice if it were otherwise, but realistically we must concede it is not. From this observation, one can proceed in two directions: like anarchists, one can claim that all governments are thereby illegitimate; alternatively, one can argue that the benefits of (some forms of) government are so substantial that government is legitimate, despite the fact that not all citizens consent to it. The second direction is surely the right one.

This has important implications for the fairness rights discussed in the previous section. Since society and its laws cannot be founded on the consent of all of its members, we have to settle for the next best thing to a consensual society, by creating a society (a democracy) the basic structure of which has the consent of the majority of its members and *deserves* the consent of all of its members. That is to say, we should create a society the basic structure of which we can reasonably ask all others to accept, even though we can predict that some unreasonable citizens will not in fact accept it. (For further discussion of this idea, see chapter 4, section 3). Since we cannot reasonably expect citizens to accept institutions that treat them in fundamentally unfair ways, this means that when governments exist at all, they must create laws that respect citizens' fairness rights.

Of course, this will hardly settle the matter as far as Machan is concerned. "Even if Duncan is right that there exist fairness rights," he might say, "it is up to citizens voluntarily to protect them, by voluntarily funding a legal system that gives citizens a fair trial, by voluntarily funding an education system that gives citizens a fair start in life, and so on." Indeed, on Machan's extreme view, even his own favored libertarian rights to security of person and property can legitimately be protected only by a police force that is funded in a voluntary fashion, rather than by tax revenues. So we must ask: Why not leave the funding of rights-protecting institutions to charity, rather than taxes? This is the subject of the following section.

4. The Insufficiency of Charity Objection

According to Machan, all taxation is "on par with forced labor" (p. 20 , quoting Robert Nozick), on a par with conscription (pp. 12, 25, and 31), or on a par with indentured servitude (pp. 24, 28, 33). A government escapes these evils only by renouncing taxation altogether and opting for a voluntary system of funding. This view, however, suffers from several severe flaws. For starters, note the numerous and obvious disanalogies between taxation and forced labor, which make any serious assimilation of the two little more than overheated rhetoric. Under a scheme of taxation, and unlike a scheme of forced labor, you get to choose what sort of career you will pursue and where you will live. You can choose whether you value material goods more than leisure time, or vice versa, and choose between more demanding and less demanding jobs accordingly. Indeed, if you are ultra-wealthy, you may not have to work at all, for you may instead live off of investment income. It surely shows a serious lack of proportion to think of some multimillionaire—who may well at this moment be sipping scotch on the deck of his yacht in the ocean waters near his second home—as anything like an indentured servant.

Putting aside Machan's overheated rhetoric, one can also object to his view on grounds of realism. This objection has two aspects. First, the current behavior of many citizens shows that it is foolish to believe that leaving things to charity will generate sufficient funds to protect citizens' rights to security and fairness. Many individuals and corporations currently exploit each loophole in existing tax law, setting up tax shelters, moving their domicile abroad, and so on.[15] What reason do we have to think that repealing all tax laws will suddenly lead these individuals, via some unprecedented conversion to civic-mindedness, to make sufficient contributions to the maintenance of government institutions? Second, it is not only the tax avoidance of current individuals that gives cause for alarm; one should also be alarmed by the behavior of many individuals in real-life economies of the past, which in a great many ways were nearer to the laissez-faire ideal than our own. For instance, two centuries ago, at the start of the Industrial Revolution, and onward until the appearance of the welfare state in the twentieth century, laws regulating workplace safety, working hours, etc., were either nonexistent or minimal at best and barely enforced. Many rich landowners and industrialists then showed themselves to be serenely indifferent to the plight of their fellow citizens, living in conspicuous luxury while masses of people suffered.

And suffer they did. In a study of Great Britain, for instance, the economic historian Roderick Floud reports that as late as 1914 "much more than half of the population lived at or close to levels at which their health was affected by the lack of food, warmth, or housing."[16] For many people—an estimated 30 percent of the population in London, for example— these health effects were serious enough to render them unable to work a normal day as adults. For those who could work, life was hard. In 1856, for instance, the average work week was sixty-five hours(!)—twelve hours a day Monday through Friday, and a half-day on Saturday. Many workers worked longer hours than these. Work, moreover, was often dangerous, with many miners dying prematurely from black lung, potters dying from lead poisoning, needle-grinders suffering from "grinder's asthma," match-factory workers becoming disfigured by phosphorous-caused "phossy-jaw," and so on.[17] It would be foolish to jeopardize the tremendous gains that have been made since the start of the Industrial Revolution by returning to a laissez-faire economic system and trusting in the charity of the well-off.

This cautionary point draws further strength from an awareness of what social scientists and philosophers call "collective action problems." Consider, for instance, the safety of factories in a libertarian regime with no workplace safety laws. Suppose you are a charitably disposed factory owner who wants to make his or her factory safe. The problem is that safety devices often cost a significant amount of money, and safe procedures may be slower at producing goods. Hence your goods will be more expensive to produce, and you will be unable to sell them as cheaply as your competitor, Joe Sleazo, who cares nothing for the safety of his workers except insofar as this affects his profit margins.[18] Thus you will likely lose sales to Joe Sleazo, forcing you eventually to choose between cutting your factory's safety standards or going out of business. In this way, then, even if you are charitably disposed to your workers, the structure of the unregulated economy may force you to lower your standards. This is the "race to the bottom," and in addition to being true of workplace safety, it is true of many other business policies. As a factory owner you may wish to pay your workers a decent wage, give them decent working hours, avoid polluting the environment, and so on, but if Joe Sleazo pays his workers subsistence wages, works them ragged, and pollutes, then decent behavior on your part may make your enterprise uncompetitive and put you out of business. What a society needs to avoid this pernicious downward spiral is a change of the rules of the game, in the form of workplace safety regulations, minimum wages laws, overtime regulations, anti-pollution laws, and so on.

Moreover, there are other collective action problems, beyond the "race to the bottom," to which libertarianism is exposed. Consider for instance Machan's insistence that all government institutions be funded by voluntary contributions rather than taxes. Problems arise for this proposal even if we restrict our attention to the institutions Machan himself approves of, namely, the legal system, police forces, and the armed forces. This is because these institutions are, in the language of economists, "public goods"—that is, goods the existence of which requires the contributions of many people but the benefits of which can be enjoyed by all people, even non-contributors.[19] If I live within the borders of the United States, for instance, I will be protected against foreign attack like every other resident, whether or not I pay money to support the armed forces. I will also benefit from the deterrence of crime created by the police force and legal system, whether or not I pay to support these institutions.

This fact creates the incentive to become a "free-rider": "If I will acquire the benefit whether I contribute or not," some people will reason, "then why contribute?" This incentive to free-ride is problematic for at least two reasons. First of all, if enough people reason in this fashion, there will be insufficient funds to supply the good. The good's existence, then, is made vulnerable or is ruled out entirely. Secondly, even if there are enough scrupulous contributors (as compared with free-riders) to fund the good, these scrupulous contributors are being exploited by the free-riders. This is bad enough in itself, but it may well have an additional bad consequence: rather than be exploited by their fellow citizens, after all, many initially civic-minded individuals may cease their own contributions in disgust—better to be a non-contributor than a sucker, they may reason—thereby further threatening the good's existence. The solution to these two problems is to make contributions compulsory, that is, to pay for the goods by taxes; this will protect the public good against the threat that free-riding poses to its existence, and it will protect contributors against exploitation. If citizens are entitled to use the law to defend their dignity against threats to their person and property, surely they can use the law to defend their dignity against threats of exploitation.

Machan trivializes this line of thought by citing examples of trivial goods. We benefit, Machan notes, from "nice looking or smelling people we walk by," (p. 21) but we owe them no money for this benefit. This is right, but the good of a nice-smelling person does not require many individuals' contributions for its provision, and more importantly, as goods go it is hardly in the same league (to put it mildly) as the good of protection against foreign invasion, murder, theft, and so on. This good of protection is of fundamental importance, as any reasonable person can recognize. The same is true of other goods of fundamental importance, such as provisions to ensure that trials are fair, votes are equally counted, access to economic opportunity is fair, and so on.

Conclusion

I have focused on four errors committed by libertarians such as Machan. First, they defend an extreme account of moral rights to property but do not anchor these rights in an adequate moral foundation. Second, despite their focus on the importance of negative liberty to human dignity, they are blind to the existence of threats to human dignity beyond intentional uses of physical force, namely, threats posed by private economic power and by social arrangements that give some people unfair access to essential goods like economic opportunity, personal security, political influence, and criminal justice. Third, it is unpersuasive to claim that rights to fair access to these goods exist only when all citizens consent to a government that recognizes such rights in its laws; if governments, to be legitimate, really needed the consent of *all* their citizens, then no feasible government would be legitimate. Fourth, it is inadequate to leave the funding of rights-protecting institutions to charity. History suggests this is unwise, and in any case people who contribute to the support of such institutions are entitled to protect themselves against exploitation by free-riders.

There are other problems with libertarianism besides these four. But these problems are enough to refute libertarianism's claim to our allegiance.

Notes

1. In this critique I will focus on the fundamental claims of libertarianism, rather than its policy implications regarding affirmative action, drug legalization, and so on. The issue of affirmative action in particular is indeed a complex one. For important defenses of it, see Ronald Dworkin, *Sovereign Virtue: The Theory and Practice of Equality* (Cambridge, Mass.: Harvard University Press, 2000), chaps. 11 and 12; and Elizabeth S. Anderson, "Integration, Affirmative Action, and Strict Scrutiny," *NYU Law Review* 77 (2002): 1195–271.

2. This is an oft-made point in the literature against libertarianism. For some references, see Fried "Left-Libertarianism: A Review Essay," *Philosophy and Public Affairs* 32 (2004), note 49. See also section 4 of chapter 6 of this book for quotations from "founding fathers" who make this very point.

3. One important disanalogy between the vendor case and the case of taxation is the fact that vendors *choose* to join the antique market on the owners' terms, whereas most citizens are *born* into the state. I will explore the implications of this important fact in section 3 below, "The Dilemma of Consent Objection."

4. This truth can be easily obscured by the terms used in sentences like, "The government taxes your earnings." For one might ask: If, as this sentence says, the earnings in questions are yours, does this not mean that you own them, and thus that government taxes do in fact confiscate money you own? The answer to this question, however, is no. Possessives like "your," "my," "his," "her," etc., do not always signify ownership. When you speak of "my mother," "my country," "my shadow," "my first kiss," and so on, you do not mean that you *own* your mother, your country, your shadow, or your first kiss (whatever that would come to!). At a general level, the phrase "your x" merely indicates that you stand in a relation to x that not everyone else in your audience stands in; this leaves it open as to whether the relation in question is one of ownership or some other relation. Legally speaking, then, the sentence "your pre-tax earnings are x" just means that you stand in a particular relation to x, namely, that this number is the amount that will be entered into the tax equations that determine how much money you legally own.

5. Moreover, where there *is* uncertainty due to a vaguely worded property law, one solution is to rewrite the law. Eliminating rather than rewriting a vague law is like treating a case of dandruff with decapitation.

6. This point is extensively explored in G. A. Cohen, *Self-Ownership, Freedom, and Equality* (Cambridge, U.K.: Cambridge University Press, 1995), chap. 2.

7. For a survey of philosophical issues related to property rights, see Lawrence Becker, *Property: Philosophic Foundations* (Boston: Routledge and K. Paul, 1977). For a critical evaluation of Robert Nozick's well-known libertarian discussion of initial acquisition (building on John Locke's theory), see Cohen, *Self-Ownership, Freedom, and Equality*, chap. 3. Indeed, the gap in argument surrounding the problem of initial acquisition has permitted the rise of "left-libertarians"—thinkers who are absolutists about owning one's own labor but who are egalitarians about the ownership of external natural resources. See Fried, "Left Libertarianism" for a recent survey of left-libertarian literature.

8. Libertarians' recognition of only a few *types* of legitimate force, however, does not mean that the *number of instances* that the libertarian state must use armed force will likewise be few, however. I wonder whether a libertarian state will need frequently to deploy anti-riot police squads to keep the unemployed and impoverished from rioting, for instance. Machan might reply that libertarianism, by permitting material inequalities that create incentives for entrepreneurs to innovate, would generate the economic growth needed to solve these problems (see for instance his claim on page 17 linking a free market with "a more prosperous society"). The relationship between material inequality and economic growth is a complex relationship, however, and one that is much debated among economists. If anything, the empirical evidence suggests a negative correlation between inequality and economic growth, due in part to the wasted human potential among the poor and uneducated. For further discussion, see Andrew Glyn and David Miliband, eds., *Paying for Inequality: The Economic Costs of Social Injustice* (London: Rivers Orem, 1994); Klaus Deininger and Lyn Squire, "Economic Growth and Income Inequality: Reexamining the Links" (1997), www.worldbank.org/fandd/english/0397/articles/0140397.htm; and the references in note 12 of Alan B. Krueger, "Inequality, Too Much of a Good Thing," unpublished manuscript available online at www.irs.princeton.edu/pubs/pdfs/inequality4.pdf.

9. Though insofar as a person's economic power depends upon the state's physical enforcement of his or her property rights, it is debatable just how separate economic power is from physical power.

10. Machan, by labeling the doctrine of positive rights "arbitrary and incoherent" (p. 28), must think that these judgments of fairness are arbitrary and incoherent. But what is the ground for this assertion? That people disagree about fairness? This ignores the broad consensus that exists regarding many forms of unfairness—cheating, racial discrimination, childhood poverty, etc. Moreover, people disagree about the limits and content of *negative rights*, too; Machan cannot think that this makes the doctrine of negative rights arbitrary and incoherent.

11. The only exceptions concern those who are necessarily dependents: children, and people who owing to profound disability are incapable of participating in the economy. For them, fair access to the means of subsistence is a right to be provided with means necessary for a decent life. (Note the misplaced emphasis involved in Machan's complaint [p. 20] that no parent has a right "to the education of his or her children." On the contrary, it is not the parents who have the right to have their children educated; it is first and foremost the children who have the right to an education.) Children, of course, will upon reaching maturity assume the correlative duty of this right, namely, a duty to support a system that gives children a fair start in life. The profoundly disabled will not. This is one case where the fairness rights I am defending take an asymmetric form—that is, are not counterbalanced with a correlative duty. I cannot see that this is an objection, however; the plight of the profoundly disabled is hardly an enviable one. As such, a complaint that the profoundly disabled are exploiting their fellow citizens does not ring true.

12. Arguably, though, Locke waffles on the issue of whether the consent of all or of just the majority is needed. See for instance John Locke, *Two Treatises of Government*, ed. Peter Laslett (Cambridge, U.K.: Cambridge University Press, 1960), 362, para. 140. For a non-libertarian interpretation of Locke generally, see A. John Simmons, *The Lockean Theory of Rights* (Princeton, N.J.: Princeton University Press, 1992), especially chap. 6.

13. John Locke, *Two Treatises of Government*, 348, para. 119.

14. David Hume, "Of the Original Contract," in *Modern Political Thought: Readings from Machiavelli to Nietzsche*, ed. David Wootton (Indianapolis, Minn.: Hackett, 1996), 387–96.

15. In 2002, for instance, American multinational companies reported a record $149 billion in profits in tax-haven countries (i.e., countries with low or no corporate taxes). "Taxing Global Profits," *New York Times*, September 17, 2004.

16. Roderick Floud, *The People and the British Economy: 1830–1914* (New York: Oxford University Press, 1997), 23. Quoted in Emmet Barcalow, *Justice, Equality, and Rights* (Belmont, Calif.: Wadsworth/Thomson Learning, 2004), 216.

17. Floud, *The People and the British Economy*, 23, 31, 78.

18. I borrow the character of Joe Sleazo from Richard B. Freeman and Kimberly Ann Elliott, *Can Labor Standards Improve under Globalization?* (Washington, D.C.: Institute for International Economics, 2003), 37. This is an example of the collective action problem known as the "Prisoner's Dilemma." For further discussion of this and other collective action problems, see Jon Elster, *Nuts and Bolts for the Social Sciences* (Cambridge, U.K.: Cambridge University Press, 1989).

19. For further discussion of public goods, see Joseph Stiglitz, *Economics* (New York: W. W. Norton, 1993), 180–82, and John Rawls, *A Theory of Justice*, rev. ed. (Cambridge, Mass.: Harvard University Press), 234–42.

3

Fairness—or Equality—
Is No Imperative

Tibor R. Machan

The idea that equality of conditions—apart from the condition that all receive equal respect and protection for their basic and derivative rights—is a sign of a good and just society is widespread and prominent among academic political thinkers, far more so than the idea that a consistent, uncompromised condition of freedom, in the sense of respect for everyone's negative rights to life, liberty—including, especially, ownership—and the pursuit of happiness, makes a society just.[1] That's to say, most academic political thinkers are egalitarians, not libertarians.

So in this last portion of my contribution to this work I wish to address the claim that fairness or equality of conditions is indeed what justice requires. It is something Professor Duncan endorses, certainly, when in outlining his own position (chapter 4) he identifies human equality as a "core value" and tells us, "If we want a fair society in which all citizens are treated as equals, we need a level training field as much as a level playing field" (p. 103). He also stresses that "a concern to respect human *equality* in addition to human freedom will lead to a concern with more than just an *adequate* opportunity to shape one's life" (p. 101).

It is not difficult to tell from our respective discussions that whereas Professor Duncan finds equality to be a core value, libertarians consider this a mistake—they consider liberty, or the right to it, the core political value of a just society. One reason they find the attempt to establish "more than just an *adequate* opportunity to shape one's life"[2] objectionable is that doing so is a serious threat to respecting and protection everyone's equal right to liberty![3]

As noted, in our time and for a couple of centuries previously many prominent political thinkers—probably most unambiguously Jean Jacques Rousseau[4]—have claimed that a very strong moral, even political, imperative is that people must be treated fairly, that they be treated as basically equal, with equal benefits and burdens for all. Among those today who promote this idea explicitly is the philosopher Kai Nielsen[5] and the even more prominent legal theorists Ronald Dworkin[6] and Cass R. Sunstein.[7]

The policy implications of this view are, for the most part, the extensive and continuous redistribution of wealth. No one has the right to keep assets, for example, that he or she came by either via hard work, good luck, or especially the voluntary payments of others via market transactions or even gifts. A beautiful model who gains considerable wealth because others wish to pay for seeing her, for example, is to be taxed extensively, and the funds taken from her are to be spread out to others who do not enjoy this advantage, who are disadvantaged. Even a very hardworking executive or tennis professional, paid a large salary because he or she has successfully put a corporation on a firm economic footing or entertained millions with his or her superb athletic prowess, may not keep these earnings but is taxed progressively—not proportionately—and the funds are to be redistributed by politically appointed bureaucrats (who are first paid for this work quite handsomely). Nor may anyone who is lucky enough, say, to win a huge amount of money in a lottery keep his or her winnings; they must be parted from a significant portion of it, and that, too, will be redistributed.[8]

All in all, the ideal of fairness or equality as espoused by its champions would not even allow the sort of differences in wealth and poverty that would remain after the familiar taxation policies of most welfare states—those policies do not go far enough, the champions argue.

There are various philosophically interesting reasons offered why this ideal really is a political imperative and why the law and public policy ought to be guided by it. One is hinted at in John Rawls's discussion, in his *A Theory of Justice*,[9] of whether people ever deserve the wealth they obtain in market transactions. He claims they do not, that none of us really earns anything, since we are all basically socially conditioned, including those of us who turn out to be hardworking, entrepreneurial individuals. Our ambition or effort really is not something we cultivate for ourselves, so we should not be rewarded for it with what we earn. It is entirely accidental who will be ambitious and who will not, so letting stand the original distribution that comes from voluntary exchanges must be unjust. The second argument rests more on intuition; many hold that it is simply natural for us all to share in the common wealth of society—that we know this to be so intuitively.[10]

The intuitionist approach is one on which I will not spend much time, other than to note that intuitions are notoriously bad guides to what we ought to be doing. To reiterate what W. Somerset Maugham pointed out, "intuition, [is] a subject upon which certain philosophers have reared an imposing edifice of surmise, but which seems to me to offer as insecure a foundation for any structure more substantial than a Castle in Spain as a ping pong ball wavering on a jet of water in a shooting gallery."[11] Intuitions are in constant flux. On their basis slavery, for example, was apparently morally and politically acceptable in one age, though not in another, and so with the abuse of women and children and prisoners of war, to name just a few areas wherein we clearly seek for moral stability but are not provided with it by intuitions. Intuitions—or as they are better known, common sense—can be an initial clue to where the truth lies, but it cannot be decisive.[12]

Another serious challenge to individualism and individual rights maintains that people are by their very nature parts of a larger whole—society, tribe, humanity, the ethnic group or the community—and so belong to a group the members of which are owed loyalty and solidarity from them. Socialists like August Comte and Karl Marx held this view, as do some contemporary communitarians like Charles Taylor. These thinkers insist that the classical liberal polity rests on the false belief in atomistic individualism. This view holds that we are independent, self-sufficient beings who can do without society altogether and for whom social relations are entirely optional. Such a view is similar to what some economists work with as they analyze market relations, but critics claim classical liberals rest all their ideas on it.[13]

This ant-colony/beehive notion of human social life gains some support from the Aristotelian idea that we are all essentially social. But to take it as far as socialists and communitarians do is an extreme leap. It denies that individuals can form ideas of their own, govern their own lives in light of these ideas, and are responsible for the result. Others should not be burdened if they live in misguided ways. Also, it is wrong to believe that we are obligated to shoulder burdens and share rewards, as if we belonged to some natural club or tribe. But fairness or equal treatment follows if we do, so this idea is often invoked to support the redistributionist state. In fact, though we are social beings, there is an essential individuality to our lives as well, and this requires for our flourishing that we enjoy sovereignty in how we live, rather than involuntary servitude to people with whom we did not choose to associate.

As such, it is not unfair at all to be better off than others— they are not owed our lives and labors by us, contrary to how egalitarians think. It is not unfair, either, that some people gain the friendship of very appealing persons while others are left loners, or that some are sought out by audiences for their talents and skills while others must fend for themselves without such enthusiastic support. The main issue of political morality is, instead, that none of this involves forcing people to do what they do not choose to do—that is, using coercion on them.[14] That is what civilized life requires, not the abolition of distinctions and differences that may yield variable advantages.

Concerning fairness or equality, one reason that these seem such ubiquitous imperatives in our time could well be that in a reasonably abundant society children grow up being treated rather fairly by parents, who owe all of them (in the family) decent treatment. Just as a teacher is supposed to attend to all of his or her students—having in effect made a promise to all of them to serve them with his or her skills—so parents have basically promised their kids to treat them equally well, provided they have the wealth to do so.[15]

But all of this is highly conditional and by no means basic—what is basic is the responsibility to keep the promise to provide service or good rearing. Yet having grown up with the justified expectation, based on the promise, of equally good treatment or fairness from parents and teachers, it makes some psychological sense that this expectation be extended to governments that claim to be providers for their citizens—not just providers of equal protection of their basic rights to be free but of whatever governments (politicians) promise (in a welfare state, for instance).[16]

Yet this expectation is misguided, for two reasons: the government is not a parent, and governments should not attempt to provide citizens with everything they would like.

The Rawlsian case is a bit more complicated, because, as we already noted, it rests on a very controversial yet widely championed idea in our time, namely, determinism. This view holds that all people behave as they must, based on the factors that impel them to do so. Be these factors genes, evolutionary forces, peer pressure, or whatever, there is a widespread idea, drawn from the extrapolation from classical physics, that none of us is free or responsible and thus deserving of either gains or losses. It is all a matter of accident.

Paradoxically, however, from this picture, based on a deterministic view of human life, a moral conclusion is drawn, one that is incompatible with determinism—that we all ought to work to fix the accidental distribution of benefits and harms, gains and losses, by means of a political order that is guided by fairness. Since "ought" implies "can," this imperative cannot be reconciled with determinism. But never mind—just as Kant believed that a deterministic (phenomenal) world coexists with a (noumenal) realm where choice is possible, so Rawls and his followers embrace this two-world picture, one in which determinism rules, another in which freely chosen moral and political conduct would remedy matters.

These last points not only indicate the paradoxical nature of the Rawlsian-based fairness imperative but also undermine it. It turns out that, after all, we are moral agents, that we can act in ways that make us more deserving, perhaps deserving even of greater wealth than what others obtain.

Furthermore, there is a non sequitur afoot in this version of the fairness imperative: that one does not deserve one's assets does not mean that others may take them away. One does not deserve a lot of things that others have no authority to take from one—say, an extra kidney, a good second eye, one's labor and talents, etc., etc.

For these reasons—among probably others that have to do with the debilitating nature of trying to implement an egalitarian regime—the fairness imperative is misguided.[17] It is also impossible, since in the effort to accomplish the massive redistribution of benefits and harms, those who take on this task obtain an inordinately greater measure of power over others than those others have. That, in turn, is the most insidious inequality or unfairness that a human community can contain.

Instead of ending on a highly abstract note, let me recount here that over the years I've written a lot about the virtue of liberty—one of my books has that as its title, in fact—yet even among many of my readers who find my arguments sound and my conclusions true there are many who do not seem to be able to shake their disdain for the rich, thinking it is quite unfair that they are so much better off then the rest of us. Even lovers of liberty often think of the rich as they might of prostitutes—sure, it's wrong to stop them, but they are an unsavory lot, aren't they?[18]

Why is this attitude toward the rich so widespread? Why do some find it so awful that certain people who can afford it take long vacations on the French or Italian Riviera and drive fancy cars and wear snappy outfits that cost a bundle even while others struggle? It is generally not some particular rich person who draws such ire, not someone who may have embezzled or otherwise illicitly gained his wealth. Not at all—it is the fact of their being rich, period.

An anecdote may be of some use here. A few summers ago I had a chance to tour Versailles, where I took a close look at the palace of Marie Antoinette and Louis the XVI.[19] A point recurred to me during this visit that I had thought of on similar visits to castles and palaces around the globe, how easily people still confuse the wealth that comes by way of conquest with wealth that is achieved. French royalty, for example, or the Habsburgs, or any other dynasty, became wealthy and spent enormous sums on luxuries not in consequences of hard work, diligence, or even simple good luck but because millions of others were kept in servitude and had their labors taken from them. Unlike, say, a Bill Gates, Warren Buffett, or the late Sam Walton, as well as many, many others who have earned and kept earning their wealth through innovation, wheeling and dealing, or other honest means, the bulk of the rich in the past gained it mainly by way of conquest and subjugation.

In the economic theories of ancient times—say, Aristotle's—it was generally believed that wealth had to be expropriated, that it was all a zero-sum process: those who gained had to make others lose. That, of course, created a widespread moral disapproval of riches, to the point that calling riches "filthy" was nearly axiomatic—if by "filth" is meant "wrongful," "nasty," or "inexcusable."

But matters have changed significantly over the years, and at least in certain parts of the world those who are wealthy can very often honestly claim to have made themselves so, apart from that little bit of luck that's always handy in such cases. Now economic prosperity, even great abundance, is more akin to other types of excellence that human beings can achieve on their own initiative—scientific or artistic achievements, even philosophical astuteness. A fabulous athlete, or a scientist or artist whose work is widely welcome and rewarded will, of course, manage to afford some very unusual perks in life—and now a fabulous financier or business genius can as well.

Even those who are somewhere in the middle class economically can afford journeys, clothing, dining, books, entertainment, and the rest that in the past only a small fraction of the human race could hope for. Still, even in our time there are millions in various regions of the world who are systemically barred from even aspiring to such prosperity as is near at hand for most North Americans, Western Europeans, Australians, and New Zealanders. But in these regions a different economic order has taken hold, albeit not without resistance, and wealth can in the case of many be attributed not to theft and expropriation but to achievement, to earning power. The rest, who are trapped in political economic systems wherein free trade and property rights are barely heard of, would still be justified in thinking of the rich in their midst as filthy, mainly because they are rich from stealing from everyone else. So, perhaps one should show a bit of understanding, if not tolerance, toward those who still live with the bad habit of regarding with suspicion everyone who is rich.[20]

Getting wealthy honestly is, then, relatively new. It may take a while before we will all consider it as clean and treat poverty as filthy—since very few of the poor will have any excuse for being poor any longer. Instead of wishing we were all in the same boat—equal in opportunity, conditions, and results—we will readily appreciate that variable circumstances are natural as well as often moral. We may learn that attempting to equalize it all can only lead to the worst type of inequality, namely, inequality of the power of some over others.

The reason is plain: Equality of conditions, even of opportunity (apart from the legally protected right to freedom to seek what one wants) is, technical philosophical considerations aside, simply quite impossible. It introduces a plethora of conflicts, inconsistencies, and problems, and it implies, ultimately, a totally socially engineered culture that can easily serve as a model of dystopia for politically geared science fiction novels.[21]

In his critique of my opening essay, Professor Duncan observes that we share a premise as we begin our defense of our respective political position, that being the basic dignity of the human individual. This is roughly right, except that built into his idea of human dignity there is in Professor Duncan's understanding room for one person's taking from another portions of his or her life and works, whereas in mine this is precluded. No one is entitled to other people's person or estate, however unfair this may seem when looked at as if these persons had some sort of covenant to share. But they do not have such a covenant, not unless they enter into one freely, uncoerced.

Notes

1. Although the ideas and ideals of laissez-faire capitalism or, more broadly, libertarianism are in sufficient circulation to be subjects of discussion and, certainly, severe criticism, the egalitarian stance is clearly the favorite of major figures in political philosophy and theory who teach at the most prestigious institutions and publishing with the most prominent presses, both commercial and university. I do not believe there can be any reasonable dispute about this.

2. Libertarians consider respecting everyone's right to liberty (and so forth) a right that is, of course, held *equally* by everyone, so there is a measure of equality in the libertarian view of justice—consider, as a case in point, that the Declaration of Independence states that we are all "created equal," just before it states, as well, that we possess "unalienable rights; that among these are life, liberty, and the pursuit of happiness." (See, for more on this, Roderick Long,

"Equality: The Unknown Ideal," at www.mises.org/fullstory.aspx? control=804.) This is the extent of egalitarianism in libertarianism. Libertarians deny, also, that individual have the right to equal opportunity—it would be wrong to attempt to engineer society for this purpose, and also quite impossible, since clearly those not involved in the engineering process would not have the equal opportunity for having things their way. Furthermore, they have argued that the assumption that one can secure both the right to equality (as in equal opportunity or equal conditions) and the right to (negative) liberty is erroneous. The attempt to secure any so-called right to equality will routinely undermine respect of the equal right to liberty of all.

3. It needs to be noted that in a discussion about political theory, not unlike theories in other disciplines, what one ought to aim for is a comparatively better position, not one that meets the impossible criterion of a final answer. No position human beings formulate could ever be final, not about substantive matters such as how a human community ought to be organized. Answers to such questions can always be modified, updated, improved upon, as new facts come to light, as the old facts may need reorganization.

4. The work that addresses the issue most directly is Jean-Jacques Rousseau, *A Discourse on Inequality*, trans. Maurice Cranston (New York: Penguin Books, 1984).

5. Kai Nielsen, *Equality and Liberty: A Defense of Radical Egalitarianism* (Totowa, N.J.: Rowman and Allanheld, 1985).

6. Ronald Dworkin, *Sovereign Virtue: The Theory and Practice of Equality* (Cambridge, Mass.: Harvard University Press, 2000).

7. Cass R. Sunstein, *The Second Bill of Rights: FDR's Unfinished Revolution and Why We Need It More Than Ever* (New York: Basic Books, 2004).

8. Professor Duncan asserts that taxation cannot be theft, since it is legal. Does this imply that the deliberate killing of Jews in the Third Reich could not have been murder, since it was legal? Instead of quibbling here, let me note that, more precisely, taxation is a form of *extortion*. It amounts to the government threatening to punish—with the possibility of killing, in the case of one's strong resistance—someone unless he or she gives up portions of his or her wealth, income, property or whatever other form the tax takes. For a detailed treatment of this matter, see Tibor R. Machan, "No Taxation, With or Without Representation," in Robert W. McGee, ed., *Taxation and Public Finance in Transition and Developing Economies* (New York: Springer, 2005). As to how a legal system can be funded without such extortion, see Tibor R. Machan, "Dissolving the Problem of Public Goods: Financing Government without Coercive Measures," in *The Libertarian Reader*, ed. T. R. Machan (Lanham, Md.: Rowman & Littlefield, 1982).

9. John Rawls, *A Theory of Justice* (Cambridge, Mass.: Harvard University Press, 1971).

10. "The assertion that a man deserves the superior character that enables him to make the effort to cultivate his abilities is . . . problematic; for his character depends in large part upon favorable family and social circumstances for which he can claim no credit." Rawls, *A Theory of Justice*, 104. If this is not a flat-out denial of free will and personal responsibility, it difficult to tell what it amounts to. Cf. David L. Norton, *Personal Destinies: A Philosophy of Ethical Individualism* (Princeton, N.J.: Princeton University Press, 1976), 328: "To my knowledge, nowhere has attention been called to the fact that egalitarianism's ubiquitous suspicion of advantage precludes to its adherents our natural delight in the presence of persons of surpassing moral excellence."

11. W. Somerset Maugham, *A Writer's Notebook* (Baltimore: Penguin, 1967), 325.

12. Intuitions are initial clues because they are unexamined but strong convictions or beliefs. They are, however, acquired haphazardly, unself-consciously, so upon scrutiny can be found to be misguided.

13. The source of this idea is the philosophy of Thomas Hobbes who, in his *Leviathan*, laid out an understanding of human beings as entirely unique and who join society as a matter of a social contract they enter. They have no human nature in line with which they conform to certain limits, and whatever limits that befall their lives are a matter of their own decision.

14. Two especially insightful works elaborate these points along classical liberal, libertarian lines: Murray N. Rothbard, *Egalitarianism as a Revolt against Nature, and Other Essays*, 2nd ed. with an introduction by David Gordon (Auburn, Ala.: Ludwig von Mises Institute, 2000), and Antony Flew, *The Politics of Procrustes: Contradictions of Enforced Equality* (Buffalo, N.Y.: Prometheus Books, 1981).

15. Within a theological framework of political justice the idea that we are all God's children also encourages the idea that whoever stands in for God on earth—say, the king or the government—owes us all care, and we in turn must share whatever burdens face humanity. Since I am operating here from a naturalist framework, I merely mention this point and do not discuss it further.

16. For a development of this point, see Tibor R. Machan, *Private Rights and Public Illusions* (New Brunswick, N.J.: Transaction Books, 1995).

17. A similar imperative is that of impartiality—so that, for example, if one has moral responsibilities toward some persons, impartiality will require that these be fulfilled toward all others (at least in reach). As Peter Unger puts it, "On pain of living a life that's seriously immoral, a typical well-off person, like you and me, *must* give away most of her financially valuable assets, and much of her income, directing the funds to lessen efficiently the serious suffering of others." Peter Unger, *Living High and Letting Die: Our Illusion of Innocence* (London: Oxford University Press, 1996) [my emphasis]. Thus we have the spectacle of some contemporary moral

philosophers advocating worldwide forcible wealth redistribution. For the libertarian this amounts to advocating involuntary servitude to all by all, an incoherent idea if there ever was one.

18. Apropos loving liberty, I should note that the negative liberty or right to it that libertarians defend is not one value among others, such as security or a healthy diet. This kind of liberty is a precondition for the pursuit of any value and is, in fact, not a value in itself but in relationship to how it makes possible the pursuit of all values. As F. A. Hayek pointed out, "That freedom is the matrix required for the growth of moral values—indeed not merely one value among many but the source of all values—is almost self-evident. It is only where the individual has choice, and its inherent responsibility, that he has occasion to affirm existing values, to contribute to their further growth, and earn moral merit." ("The Moral Element in Free Enterprise," in Mark W. Hendrickson, ed., *The Morality of Capitalism* [Irvington-on-Hudson, N.Y.: Foundation for Economic Education, 1992], originally written for *The Freeman*, 1962.)

For a discussion of the nature of such liberty, between two libertarians with somewhat different approaches to the issue, see Tibor R. Machan and John O. Nelson, *A Dialogue, Partly on Political Liberty* (Lanham, Md.: University Press of America, 1990).

19. Actually, while the palace was unbelievably vast and sumptuous, it is often noted that the queen and the king were a rather economically minded pair, compared to others of their class, and it was not they but the nobility in France that stood in the way of various financial reforms that would have been to the benefit of the entire country.

20. We might think of it along these lines, also: Suppose in the past someone's beauty or good constitution had been achieved by depriving others of something belonging to them. But in time these assets were either come by naturally, or with the efforts of those who possessed them. That there are still those who resent the beauty or good constitution of others could perhaps be appreciated because most people still believe these have been the result of oppression, extortion, or conquest.

21. Such works do actually exist—for example, Kurt Vonnegut, "Harrison Bergeron," in *Welcome to the Money House* (New York: Bantam Doubleday, 1988); Ayn Rand, *Anthem* (Los Angeles: Pamphleteers, 1946); and, of course, the classic George Orwell, *Animal Farm* (New York: Harcourt, Brace, 1946).

PART II

4

Democratic Liberalism: The Politics of Dignity

Craig Duncan

For the medieval philosopher St. Thomas Aquinas, the idea of hell posed one hell of a problem. He revered the Bible, of course, and the Bible says that punishment should fit the crime—as the famous phrase has it, "an eye for an eye, a tooth for a tooth." Yet the horrors of hell last forever, making hell an *infinitely bad* punishment. Wouldn't hell, then, be a fitting response *only* to an *infinitely bad* crime? But—and here is the problem—how could any finite human being possibly be guilty of such a crime?

Here is Aquinas's answer: "Sin which is committed against God is infinite. For the sin is the more serious, as the person against whom one sins is the greater. For example, it is a more serious sin to kill a prince than to kill a private citizen. But the greatness of God is infinite. Therefore, one deserves infinite punishment for a sin that is committed against God."[1] In short, when a person commits a crime, we are to measure the seriousness of that crime with reference to the "greatness" of the party wronged by the crime. Since God's greatness is infinite, an offense against God counts as an infinite crime.

To be sure, Aquinas's answer has its problems (for one thing, it implies that the average murderer's crime is on a par

79

with Hitler's crime—both are infinitely bad!). But that is neither here nor there, for this is not an essay on theology but on political philosophy. Aquinas's answer is worth examining even in an essay on political philosophy because it contains an idea with political implications that are worth exploring, namely, the idea of wronging a being's "greatness." "Greatness" is one of many such words Aquinas could have used to express his idea; other similar words include "honor," "majesty," "augustness," "magnificence," "sublimity," and—to use a word that will figure prominently in the pages to come—"dignity." This allows us to redescribe Aquinas's idea in different terms. When Aquinas says that the ultimate crime is to sin against God's greatness, we might say he means that the ultimate crime is to fail to show due respect for the dignity of God.

Aquinas's main focus is on God, but he also mentions princes and private citizens, and it is here we can discern the political implications of his idea. They are not appealing implications, for they are mired in the distinctly unappealing political assumptions of the Middle Ages. It is a greater crime, Aquinas says, to kill a prince than it is to kill a private citizen. In fact, this medieval idea of "greater dignity, greater crime" was explicitly formalized in feudal Anglo-Saxon England in the institution of the *wergild*. The wergild fixed the value of each person's life: a serf's wergild was less than a noble's wergild, which in turn was less than a king's wergild. If you killed someone, the law required you to pay that person's wergild. As Marilyn McCord Adams comments, "On this system, someone might be able to afford to kill a serf, but not a noble, or a noble but not a king. . . . [G]uilt was proportional to the augustness or majesty of the offended party and not just to the act of the offence."[2]

Fortunately, times have changed. If you respond in horror to the wergild system, then to that extent you have internalized an egalitarian idea of first-order importance, namely, the idea of the *equal dignity* of human beings. It is this egalitarian idea that lies at the foundation of the political philosophy defended in this chapter, which I will call "democratic liberalism." To that defense I now turn.

1. Dignity and Responsible Choice

Let us begin by exploring the idea of dignity. Consider a thought experiment described by the American philosopher William James. In a discussion of utopian political visions, James poses the following question:

> If the hypothesis were offered us of a world in which [various thinkers'] utopias should be all outdone, and millions kept permanently happy on the one simple condition that a certain lost soul on the far-off edge of things should lead a life of lonely torture, what except a specific and independent sort of emotion can it be which would make us immediately feel, even though an impulse arose within us to clutch at the happiness so offered, how hideous a thing would be its enjoyment when deliberately accepted as the fruit of such a bargain?[3]

I suggest that the "emotion" to which James refers is surely none other than that of respect, namely, respect for the dignity of that "certain lost soul" whose torture would guarantee the happiness of millions. The power of this idea of dignity is apparent from the size of the benefit—unimaginable happiness—that is foregone in its name.

What is it, though, that gives a human being such a powerful dignity? The most plausible answer looks to our impressive mental capabilities: our self-consciousness, our capacity to imagine future consequences, to articulate our values, to deliberate as to which course of action is best, to guide our choices by these deliberations, and so on.[4] This is a plausible answer, because this constellation of mental capabilities allows adult human beings to cross an important threshold, namely, the threshold that separates beings who are *morally responsible* for their actions from beings who are not. The powers of choice that ordinary human adults possess are such that they are responsible for their choices in a way that young children, for instance, are not. That is a significant difference, well worthy of a deep respect. This fact is acknowledged in the numerous distinctions we draw between appropriate ways of treating adults and appropriate ways of treating children. "Show me some respect," a young adult might say to her elders who persist in treating her as a not-yet-responsible being.

Of course, a number of puzzles accompany the notion of moral responsibility. Where exactly should we draw the line between beings who are responsible for their actions and beings who are not? Moreover, insofar as moral responsibility is widely thought to depend on the existence of a free will, we face the well-known challenge of how free will can exist in a world of atoms and energy bound by scientific laws. Clearly, it would be foolish of me to attempt to solve this deep challenge in the short space I have here. Instead I will be content to note that regardless of the puzzles that abound in the debate over free will, it is hard to deny that there is surely *some* difference between adults and children that warrants us treating them differently. Adult decision making is typically competent in the way a young child's simply is not. The capacity for this sort of competent decision making is what I have in mind when I speak of the capacity for responsible choice. The free-will debate, however it turns out, will surely not erase all morally relevant distinctions between adults and children.

In proposing that politics be founded on respect for human dignity, understood in terms of the distinctive human capacity for choice, I am aligning myself with a long-standing tradition in moral philosophy, the best-known adherents of which range from the ancient Greek and Roman Stoics to the eighteenth-century German philosopher Immanuel Kant and beyond.[5] I will later have more to say about Kant's position in particular. For now, though, I want to continue to develop this foundation for politics. Toward that end, the next obvious question to ask is this: Supposing the source of human dignity does lie in our capacity for responsible choice, what does it mean to *respect* this capacity? The answer to this is threefold: one respects the capacity for responsible choice by observing a strong presumption against impairing it, against constraining it, and against ignoring it (that is, against failing to recognize its existence).[6] Each of these ways of failing to respect dignity requires commentary. The next section takes up this task.

2. Respecting Human Dignity

The most devastating way one can fail to respect another person's dignity is by failing to recognize any presumption against *impairing* that person's capacity for responsible choice. In general, one impairs a person's capacity for responsible choice by crippling the mental capabilities necessary for responsible agency or by preventing their healthy development. Certain forms of abuse, both physical and psychological, can produce this result, especially if the victim is a child. Quite plausibly, too, a person's capacity for responsible choice is crippled while he or she is in the grip of a severe substance addiction. Additionally, one can impair other people's capacity for choice by paralyzing them with fear or by incapacitating them with intense and prolonged pain—and so on. In all these cases the implications for dignity are especially severe. For when a person's capacity for responsible choice is destroyed, we may say that his or her dignity is correspondingly *diminished*.[7]

The second way in which one can fail to respect another person's dignity is by failing to observe any presumption against *constraining* the exercise of that person's capacity for responsible choice. The clearest case of this lies in physical constraints on a person's body. At the extreme, the person is shackled to a dungeon wall, thereby removing nearly all opportunity for action. A prison cell allows a greater scope of action than a set of shackles but drastically less scope than exists outside of prison—and so on for other less confining physical restraints. In the case of constraint, it is not genuinely apt to say that the constrained person's dignity is *diminished*, for unlike the case of impairment, the person's capacity for responsible choice will remain intact so long as the constraint is not so extreme as to be mentally incapacitating. Rather, the harm of constraint lies in preventing the person from using this capacity in significant ways. This is a serious harm, for ideally one's life should reflect one's dignity, much like the moon reflects the light of the sun. While constrained, however, a person's life does not reflect his or her capacity for responsible choice, much like the moon no longer reflects any light while in the earth's shadow during a lunar eclipse. For this reason, it is best not to say the person's dignity is *diminished,* as we did in the previous case of impairment; rather, we should say that the person's dignity is *obscured.*

In addition to *physical* constraints, there is another important sort of constraint by which one may obscure another person's dignity, namely, *threat-based* constraints. The paradigm instance of this type of constraint is a mugger with a gun in his hand who says, "Your money or your life." Complying with his demand, you might later say, "He forced me to hand over my wallet; I had no choice but to do as he said." Of course, in a technical sense this is not quite right: you *could* have made a dash for it, or tried to tackle the mugger, or defiantly said to him, "No, you'll just have to shoot me if you want my money." From this technical point of view, the mugger does not constrain you unless and until he does so physically. We should however ask why, contrary to this technical point, it seems so natural to say that you were *forced* to do as the mugger said, even if no shot was ever fired. It is natural to say that you were forced to hand over your money, despite having some choice in a technical sense, because owing to the lethal threat against your life you had no "real" choice, we might say. Your choice was between handing over your wallet or putting your life in serious jeopardy; those were your only options. Since the latter option is an intolerable one, handing over the money was your only *tolerable* option. Given this, no one could reasonably hold you responsible for the loss of the money; your exercise of responsible choice was constrained during the mugging. During that time, your dignity was obscured—eclipsed, we might say, by the dark shadow of the mugger's deed.

This discussion of constraining a person's exercise of responsible choice helps us to understand one of our core values, namely, the value of *freedom*. This is so because constraints on people's exercise of their powers of choice are in fact constraints on their freedom. It thus follows that respect for a person's dignity requires one to respect that person's freedom. There is yet more that respect for dignity requires. For in addition to underlying the core value of human freedom, I now will argue that the ideal of respect for human dignity also underlies the core value of human *equality*.

The key question to ask about the value of equality is: In what sense are people equal? The answer to this question is hardly obvious; after all, some people are stronger than others, some are smarter, virtuous, better looking, more artistic, more personable, and so on. The ideal of respect for human dignity has an answer to this question, however. Recall the mental prerequisites of responsible choice mentioned earlier: our self-consciousness, our capacity to imagine future consequences, to articulate our values, to deliberate as to which course of action is best, to act on our choices, and so on. To be sure, people differ in each of these mental abilities; some are better than others at imagining future consequences, or at guiding their choices by their deliberations, etc. Yet once a person's degree of these abilities passes a certain threshold, we rightly hold him or her to be capable of responsible choice. That is to say, all those who pass a basic line of competency share the status of "responsible being," even if some are more competent than others. (Compare the class of responsible beings with the class of pregnant women—all of the women in this class are pregnant, even though some are more advanced in their pregnancy than others.)[8] Importantly, this is *not* to say all members of this class *do* in fact make choices we judge to be wise, prudent, moral, etc.; many do not. Rather, it *is* to say that members of this class make choices—good or bad—for which we can properly hold them responsible.

On this account of equality, one respects another person as an equal by recognizing in one's actions the other person's status as a being capable of responsible choice. Failing to do this is another failure of respect for human dignity, alongside impairing a person's capacity for responsible choice, or constraining its exercise. One fails to recognize other people's status as beings capable of responsible choice when one treats them as something other than such a being. Consider in this regard the famous formula of Kant, according to which you should "always treat humanity, whether in your own person or in the person of any other, never simply as a means, but always at the same time as an end."[9] Suppose for instance (to take one of Kant's own examples) that I borrow some money from another person and make a lying promise to repay it, with no intention ever to do so. In this case I am surely not treating the other as a person in her own right, with her own life to lead and own choices to make; rather I am treating her as nothing more than, say, an ATM machine with buttons I may push to obtain free money.

So treating others as mere instruments for achieving your personal ends is one way of failing to recognize others as responsible beings, and thus one way of failing to treat them as equals. Moreover, treating others as mere instruments is not the only way of failing to treat them as equals (that is, of failing to treat them as "ends," to use the Kantian lingo). You might for instance treat them as pieces of refuse to be destroyed or cleared away (as in cases of "ethnic cleansing"). Or you might treat them paternalistically, as incompetent at making their own choices—say, by censoring what they read, or by assigning them their occupation, choosing their spouses for them, etc. Or you might treat them as nothing at all, as nonentities. You would do this, for instance, if you look upon other people who are suffering impairment of their capacity for responsible choice, or a constraint on its exercise, and you treat them with indifference despite being able to help them with only a reasonable level of effort on your part. Finally, you might in light of a stereotype view other people as beings whose choices are fated to take a certain form; in this case you are treating others as mere cardboard cutouts of people, not full-blooded ones. In short (and at the cost of some linguistic infelicity), we can say that respecting people's capacity for responsible choice requires that we observe a very strong presumption against treating people in instrumentalizing, refusizing, infantilizing, nonentitizing, or stereotyping ways—that is, against treating them as inferiors, rather than as equals who are capable of responsible choice.

To fail to observe this presumption, we may say, is to insult another person's dignity, and hence to fail to respect it. Thus we may set *insulting* other people's dignity alongside the other failures of respect previously examined: *diminishing* other people's dignity by impairing their capacity for responsible choice, and *obscuring* other people's dignity by constraining their exercise of this capacity. Much of the rest of this chapter will be an exploration of the political implications of the strong presumption against these ways of failing to respect human dignity.

3. The Liberal Principle of Legitimacy

So far we have focused on the dignity of the human *individual*, which has led to an understanding of the freedom and equality of individuals. But of course, human individuals live in *societies*. This is surely part of our nature; as Aristotle famously said, humans are social animals.[10] In fact, our capacity for responsible choice itself requires nurturing social relations for its development. Young children who through some misfortune are forced to grow up on their own in the woods—"feral children," as they are called—are hardly recognizable as human, so irreparably diminished are their linguistic and other cognitive skills.[11] It is time, then, that we considered what implications the ideal of respect for dignity has for the way we ought to organize our societies.

The first question to ask is what society is. I propose we understand society as a system of cooperation by which members gain in their ability to complete the fundamental tasks of living. Certainly, compared to a solitary existence, life in society better enables one to feed, clothe, shelter, and protect oneself from nature's threats. The enablement that social cooperation makes possible need not be limited to enabling us in meeting our basic needs, however. Whatever goals one has *beyond* meeting one's basic needs, the resources (both physical and human) that cooperation generates will better enable one to meet those goals, compared with a Robinson Crusoe–style existence (and even Crusoe, remember, was raised in human society). These same resources will also better enable one to fulfill whatever basic moral duties one has (these too ought to be reckoned tasks of living).

This system of social cooperation should be one that respects the dignity of its members. This is easier said than done, however, for a fundamental dilemma arises in this regard. For societies of more than a handful of people, after all, cooperation requires authoritative rules; the history of human experience is testament to this fact. Moreover, in a world of less than perfect beings, these rules will need to be enforced via some sanctions, especially when there is potential for serious conflicts of interest. In general, sanctions against uncooperative behavior can take many forms, as a glance at various forms of cooperation shows. Examples include the withdrawal of good will (if you refuse to buy a round of beers when your turn comes, you will not get invited out again), penalties assigned by referees in sports,[12] the withdrawal of privileges (disbarring lawyers, removing medical licenses, etc.), and the fines and imprisonment meted out by criminal law. These last sorts of sanctions most acutely raise the dilemma I have in mind. Imprisonment and heavy fines, after all, constrain people's exercise of their capacity for responsible choice. Moreover, insofar as punishment of this sort makes some people (the punished) subordinate to others (the punishers), it is in danger of failing to recognize other people as beings who are competent to make their own choices.

The fundamental dilemma of human dignity, then, is this: On the one hand, as the case of feral children shows, the human capacity for responsible choice requires some sort of society for its development; yet on the other hand, society requires authoritative rules, the enforcement of which both constrains people's exercise of their capacity for responsible choice (thus threatening their freedom) and risks failing to recognize people as beings capable of responsible choice (thus threatening their equality). Put in terms of dignity, we may express the fundamental dilemma as this: Human dignity is diminished outside of society, and yet in society it risks being obscured or insulted.

How, then, can we reconcile the binding rules necessary for life in society with respect for human dignity—in particular, with respect for other people as free and equal beings? This puzzle is especially acute for political society, since in the typical case (immigration being the exception) one is simply born into the society in which one lives. Unlike the case, say, in which a group of friends all agree to play basketball, there does not appear to be any voluntary act in which all citizens consent to the rules of their society.[13] I believe the best response to the fundamental dilemma of human dignity is to follow the twentieth-century philosopher John Rawls and recommend that society be ordered along the lines of what he calls "the liberal principle of legitimacy." According to this principle, political decisions are legitimate insofar as they are conducted in accordance with a constitution the essentials of which it is reasonable to expect all citizens to accept as free and equal citizens.[14] This means the basic rules of society should be chosen so as to create a reasonable balance among the various inevitable threats to human dignity, chief among which are the threats of constraint and insult.

Begin first with the threat of constraints. Here it is important to realize that because not all choices a person might make are equally significant—some choices are much more fateful than others—it follows that not all constraints on choice are equally significant. In particular, it is not reasonable to expect citizens to accept a distribution of constraints that significantly constrains the fateful choices of their lives—the choice of occupation, of spouse, of friends; the choice whether to have children; and so on. By contrast, lesser constraints, such as reasonable taxes, red lights at intersections, anti-pollution laws, and so on, will leave citizens largely free to choose the shape of lives. This suggests that in asking what set of basic social rules it is reasonable to expect citizens to accept, one key criterion is whether proposed sets of rules are likely to leave citizens with a tolerable amount of choice over the shape of their lives.

This is key, for absent such choice a person's mode of life becomes that of a mere creature of circumstance; his or her dignity is obscured, and hence his or her life is degraded. The choice over the shape of one's life, moreover, must be a *real* one, in the sense explored above when discussing the case of mugging. It will not do, for instance, for a totalitarian state to say, "Well, our citizens do in fact have a *choice* of their lives' shape—a choice between the gulag and conformity." Likewise, consider an impoverished worker who lives on the edge of disaster and must constantly face "choices" in which all but a handful of options have intolerable consequences: do this or face hunger, do this or face illness, do this or face eviction, do this or see your children suffer, and so on. Since her existence is merely one of lurching from crisis to crisis, she has no significant choice over the shape of her life. Although her exercise of her capacity for responsible choice is not as constrained as that of gulag prisoner's, it is significantly constrained all the same. We might say that while gulag prisoners and impoverished workers are of course alive, they are not living much of a life.[15] To actively live a life requires at least a tolerable amount of choice among sets of tolerable options. Hence we can say this about the threat to dignity that comes with the constraints that life in society imposes on a person's freedom: In choosing basic rules that it is reasonable to expect all citizens to accept, one key criterion is whether they leave citizens with genuine choices over the shape of their lives.

What, though, about the second threat to dignity identified above, the threat to citizens' equality? This was the risk inherent in any distinction between the rulers and the ruled, namely, the risk of failing to recognize citizens' status as beings capable of leading their own lives via their capacity for responsible choice. The proper response to this threat surely lies in some form of democracy, which gives citizens an equal share of voting power, thereby recognizing in a significant way their equal status as beings capable of responsible choice. By contrast, to live under a dictatorship (even a benevolent one) and be given no say as to who rules and what laws they create is not to live as a competent adult who can order his or her own affairs. Rather, it is to live as a schoolboy or schoolgirl, in thrall to those in authority, and with little or no recourse to challenge their dictates. The line of argument from respect for dignity to democratic government is thus straight and short.

Putting this element of democracy together with the goal of leaving citizens free to shape their lives gives us a response to the fundamental dilemma of human dignity; we can conclude that society's basic social rules should establish a *liberal democracy*—that is, a democratic form of government limited by a constitutionally guaranteed set of individual rights that ensure one has significant freedom to choose the shape of one's life. The dignity-based political philosophy that recommends this form of government I will refer to as *democratic liberalism*. As with any political philosophy, however, much depends on the details. What precise form should democracy take, and precisely which rights should be guaranteed? I will consider each of these questions in turn, beginning with individual rights.

4. The Dignity-Based Conception of Rights

We can group individual rights into civil rights, personal rights, economic rights, and political rights. Basic *civil rights* include rights to freedom of expression, freedom of association, and freedom of conscience.[16] Basic *personal rights* include a right to bodily integrity (which encompasses more specific rights against slavery and against cruel punishment, as well as rights against murder and assault) and a right to privacy. The right to privacy is a complex one that encompasses more specific rights against unreasonable searches and seizures, as well as rights to choose the form of one's intimate relations, for example. These latter rights include a strong presumption against interfering with a person's choices regarding friends, sexual relations, and children (whether to have children at all, and if so, how to raise them). Basic *economic rights* include the right to hold personal property and make contracts on equal terms with others (a right formerly denied to wives, who in the past could only hold property in their husband's name) and rights against discrimination (as a job-seeker, employee, or consumer). Basic *political rights* include the equal right to vote and run for office; rights against discrimination in public services (education, government benefits, etc.); and such due process rights as the right to equality before the law and the right to contest any charges against one in a fair and timely trial.

This is a long list of rights. Moreover, each right on the list has a complex structure; books discussing them fill library shelves, and in the space I have here I cannot hope to argue for any of them in detail. What I hope instead to do is indicate in outline form how the understanding of human dignity—and in particular, the understanding of human freedom and equality that follows from this, which I have called democratic liberalism—supports these rights. Take freedom of expression as a case in point. Some of the argument for this is admittedly of a purely instrumental character. For example, it may be dangerous to entrust a government with even a limited power to censor speech, for once having this taste of power, those in charge may tyrannically seek ever more. Moreover, freedom of expression is needed to promote the vigorous public debate on which democracy relies. These are powerful arguments, but I do not think they exhaust the case for freedom of expression. The latter argument would offer little protection to nonpolitical forms of expression. The former argument risks overestimating, in paranoid fashion, the prospects of governmental tyranny. In addition, I fail to see how a very general worry about tyranny can generate a specific account of several necessary limits to freedom of expression (such as restrictions on libel, which I will discuss in a moment).

Fortunately, not all of the argument for the right to freedom of expression is of an instrumental nature. This right gains obvious intrinsic support from considerations of dignity, and its emphasis on the importance of an ability to give shape to one's life. Censors, after all, may deprive a person of valuable information she needs in shaping her life. In cases of significant state control of information, it is the *state* that significantly shapes citizens' lives, rather than citizens shaping their own lives. Moreover, since a person's conception of her fundamental moral duties is among the most important of contours in the shape of her life, it follows that insofar as these duties require her to speak or express herself in other ways, freedom of expression is a necessary element of her ability to shape her life. (Think in this regard of a religious person who believes that God requires her to be a "witness" to religious truth and evangelize on its behalf, or think of a person who believes that he has a fundamental moral duty to speak out against serious injustices of which he is aware.) For such people, limits on expression will be experienced as limits on their ability to shape their lives in fundamental ways.[17]

Considerations of human equality also support freedom of expression. In general, the ideal of respecting humans as equals translates into the political sphere as an ideal of *equal citizenship*; laws and social practices should not distinguish between first- and second-class members of society. Instead the mass of citizens should be recognized as competent adults who are themselves capable of making responsible choices. That is to say, authorities should presume each adult citizen to be capable of responsible choice. This presumption may not be true in every case; some adult citizens indeed may be so imprudent that they fail to qualify as competent at leading their own lives. Government laws are necessarily general in scope, however, rather than tailored to each individual citizen, and in general adult citizens are competent to lead their own lives.[18] A society in which government censors decide what the general public can and cannot read or hear, however, is not a society in which the mass of citizens are recognized as competent adults. Instead the censors view the mass of citizens as immature beings who must for their own good be protected from sources of expression that might corrupt them or otherwise harm them. In short, a censoring society is one that infantilizes most of its members; by failing to recognize its members' capacity for responsible choice, such a society thereby insults its members' dignity.[19]

The right to freedom of expression does, though, have limits. For instance, in the United States the Supreme Court has rightly judged that consistent with the right to freedom of expression the state may criminalize speech that is both intended to and likely to create "imminent lawless action," such as incitement to riot.[20] A proper understanding of the right to freedom of expression would recognize other exceptions as well. Examples of these include: reasonable constraints on defamation (*libel*, in written form; *slander*, in verbal form); restrictions on material that may harm minors (e.g., daytime TV/radio broadcasts and billboards of a sexually or violently graphic nature); restrictions on speech that creates a hostile work environment (e.g., sexual harassment); laws against passing on classified information or printing words in violation of a copyright; and laws against false or misleading advertising.

In each of these cases, the nature of the restrictions is to be determined by asking what restrictions it would be reasonable to expect free and equal members of society to accept. Take libel law for instance. Leaving this as a private tort (i.e., the subject of a private lawsuit) rather than a public criminal offense takes the government out of the censorship business, thereby avoiding the equality-based worries of infantilizing treatment. As for the freedom-based worries regarding restrictions on expression, here a reasonable balance must be struck between various burdens on people's ability to control the shape of their lives, and burdens that fall in different places with different sorts of libel laws. If the harm of libel is not legally recognized at all, for instance, people will lose important control over their reputations, for these will be highly vulnerable to the spread of false and malicious rumors. This is a real harm, inasmuch as some control of one's reputation is crucial for control of one's life more generally. On the other hand, too severe a penalty for libel and too loose a definition of it will significantly impede the flow of important information, as the fear of a libel suit will lead some people with important information to keep their mouths shut. As remarked above, people need a free flow of information in order to plan their lives effectively, so this is a significant burden. Inasmuch as there are burdens at stake with either the presence or absence of libel law, a reasonable compromise clearly is needed. The current U.S. understanding is a plausible compromise along these lines. According to this understanding, a party who takes offense at a published claim and sues for libel must prove that the writer knew the published claim was false or otherwise acted with a reckless disregard for the truth.[21] This understanding of libel offers potential victims protection against the most serious threats to their reputations at the hands of unscrupulous malefactors while at the same time offering competent journalists reasonable assurance against a lawsuit.

This discussion of the right to freedom of expression indicates the manner in which other individual rights are justified. The decisions protected by the right to privacy, for instance, are some of life's most fateful ones, and ones that typically lie at the heart of a person's self-understanding—hence a fundamental concern with people's ability to give shape to their lives leads to a fundamental concern with protecting privacy. The right against economic discrimination protects one against artificial obstacles that compromise one's ability to choose an occupation (a fateful decision) as well as earn the resources one in general needs to shape a life. Additionally, economic discrimination can create a castelike distinction between first- and second-class members of society; thus it is obviously objectionable on the grounds of equality as well (I will have more to say about this shortly). And so on for the other rights.

Having briefly discussed liberal rights, I want to turn now to the other half of democratic liberalism and discuss what sort of democracy the ideal of respect for human dignity requires.

5. Improving Democracy

As with individual rights, the issues related to the structure of democracy are complex ones, and my remarks will have to be suggestive. One important question concerns whether to have a *direct* democracy (in which citizens themselves propose and vote on laws) or a *representative* democracy (in which elected offices perform these functions). To a large extent this question is settled by pragmatic considerations (direct democracies are better suited to small city-states than to today's large nation-states), but a dignity-based case is not wholly silent here. I do not believe that the demands of dignity *require* direct democracy, for to say that citizens are competent beings capable of responsible choice is not to say they are all competent to judge the various issues requiring political attention, from taxes to defense to education to the environment and so on. A representative democracy instead, and more accurately, presumes citizens are first and foremost competent to choose leaders who are themselves competent at judging these issues. This is not to say that the ideal of direct democracy has no relevance, however. Since in fact many private citizens do have competent knowledge of a variety of issues, especially those that directly implicate their interests, a representative democracy should also create significant space for citizen input into its deliberative practices (via open hearings and other public forums, say).[22]

In addition to the choice between direct and representative democracy, other important choices concern the structure of political elections and campaigns. Regarding elections, one important choice is that between "winner-take-all" electoral systems and systems of "proportional representation." In a winner-take-all system of voting, such as exists in the United States, the candidate with the highest number of votes is elected, and no one else. The major disadvantage of this system is that it easily leads to a political scene in which two parties dominate, making it extremely hard for smaller parties to arise and win office. (Think, for instance, of how hard it is to get elected in the United States if one is not a member of the Republican or Democratic parties.) This is so because many voters will see a third-party vote as a wasted one, given the dim prospects of electoral success.

By contrast, most European democracies have an electoral system of "proportional representation," which allows a greater variety of parties to win legislative office. Although such systems can be structured in different ways,[23] one example of such a structure will indicate the general idea. A legislative district in this structure is not a small district with *one* representative, as in the current U.S. system for the House of Representatives, but rather a larger district with (say) five representatives. Each party then fields up to five candidates for the district. Correspondingly, each voter has five votes to spread among the candidates as he or she pleases (including the option of multiple votes on a particularly favored candidate). Once the votes are counted the top five vote-getters receive legislative seats. Such a system, unlike our current one, gives small parties a realistic chance of winning a seat, for any candidate receiving over 20 percent of the vote is guaranteed election, and in races with many participants a candidate can often win with less than this. This is likely to enrich public debate by including a greater diversity of viewpoints, which in turn is likely to improve the quality of debate and thereby improve the quality of laws and public policies. A second benefit, and one that is even more significant from the point of view of democratic liberalism, is that proportional representation is more truly representative, inasmuch as the views of legislators will more closely mirror the actual spectrum of views that prevail among citizens. This reduces the gap between the ruling group and the ruled, and thereby better respects the dignity of citizens.

Beyond the choice of electoral systems, another important choice in the design of democracy is the choice of campaign systems. An important question here is what role money ought to play. In the United States, the amount of money involved in politics is staggering. According to data from the Federal Elections Commission, for instance, the average cost of all campaigns for the U.S. House of Representatives in 2002 was nearly $468,000. More particularly, the average cost of a winning House campaign was $898,000; the average cost of defeating an incumbent was $1.6 million.[24] In the 2000 House races, 94 percent of the candidates who spent the most money won.[25] Running for the U.S. Senate, moreover, is even more costly. For Senate races in 2002, the average cost of all campaigns was $2.2 million, the average cost of a winning campaign was $4.8 million, and the average cost of defeating an incumbent was $6.8 million.[26] In the 2000 Senate races, 85 percent of the candidates who spent the most money were successful at the polls.[27] In the 2004 presidential election George W. Bush spent $367 million, compared to John Kerry's $323 million.[28]

The obvious threat here is that our system is becoming (has become?) merely a democracy in name and truly a *plutocracy* in practice (plutocracy being rule by the wealthy). The system is broken, and in general politicians are not nearly as responsive to the needs of everyday people as they should be. As things stand now, the huge amounts of money involved in politics give wealthy citizens (and large corporations) wildly disproportionate political influence, in terms of access both to politicians and to political office itself.[29] This is obviously incompatible with any reasonable conception of equal citizenship, for the point of an equal right to vote is subverted when dollars rather than votes are the driving force in the formation of law and policy.

What can we do to fix this? Something is needed to give nonwealthy candidates a fair chance of obtaining office, and to free them once elected from the need to indebt themselves to wealthy campaign donors. Fortunately, one such remedy is already in place in Maine, Arizona, Vermont, North Carolina, Massachusetts, and New Mexico—namely, the "Clean Money, Clean Elections" system of public campaign finance. This system is a voluntary one—that is, it is a candidate's choice whether or not to participate in the Clean Elections system. Candidates who wish to participate must qualify by collecting a set number of five-dollar donations from voters in their district. A candidate running for the Arizona House, for example, must collect two hundred of these five-dollar donations. Once qualified, candidates must not spend any private money, including their own; instead each receives a fixed amount of campaign funding based upon previous campaign averages in their state. Sticking with the example just used, an Arizona House candidate receives ten thousand dollars for the primary and fifteen thousand for the general election. Additionally, if a Clean Elections candidate is outspent by a privately funded opponent, then funds matching the private candidate's expenditures are released to the Clean Elections candidate. Independent expenditures can also trigger matching funds (e.g., if, say, MoveOn.org funds advertisements for liberal candidates or the NRA funds advertisements for conservative candidates). These matching funds are not limitless—in Arizona, for instance, matching funds are capped at triple the original grant amount—but in practice they have worked well to give publicly funded candidates competitive shots at gaining office.[30]

While this system has only been in place since 2000 in Maine and Arizona (and not even that long in other states), it is already a tremendous success. In Arizona, for instance, there was a 58 percent increase in the number of people who ran in the 2000 election cycle compared with the 1996 cycle. Clean Elections candidates now hold 41 percent of all statewide offices.[31] Voter turnout in 2002 was 22 percent higher than in

1998.[32] The number of minority candidates tripled between 1998 and 2002.[33] Also, while of course the system requires tax-payer money, the amount required is affordable—$12.9 million in Arizona in the 2002 elections, for example[34]—and it is money well spent, inasmuch as it preserves the health of our democracy. Like health care for individuals, we should not in any case expect health care for democracy to be cost-free.

6. Opportunity for Free and Equal Workers

So far we have discussed the forms of individual rights and democratic governance that it would be reasonable to expect members of society to accept as free and equal people. These subjects were worth discussing because of the far-reaching implications they have for the freedom and equality of soci-ety's members. Another subject that needs discussing is the structure of the economy, for this too has far-reaching impli-cations for the freedom and equality of society's members. A full discussion of this subject would evaluate various capital-ist and socialist ways of structuring the economy. Limited space precludes a full discussion, however; my strategy in-stead is to examine the system that readers are presumably most familiar with—namely, capitalism of the sort that pre-vails in the United States—and ask whether this system is compatible with respect for human dignity, and if not, whether it can be made so.

The first point to make is a negative one. The account of human freedom central to democratic liberalism focuses on people's ability to give shape to their own lives. This account will surely lead to an endorsement of *some* form of property rights, since control of the shape of one's life requires the con-trol of some significant amount of personal resources (one's residence, means of transport, clothing, money for raising a family, money for vacations and hobbies, etc.). This account, though, does not lead to an endorsement of *absolute* property rights, according to which nearly all forms of taxation and all limits on freedom of contract count as illegitimate restrictions on freedom. Absolute property rights are not necessary in order for people to be able to shape their lives. Property and contract rights are not currently absolute in the United States, for instance; we must pay taxes and heed business regulations. Yet it would be preposterous to suppose on this account that no one in the United States has adequate ability to give shape to his or her life. Millions of people have this ability, and have it in spades.

A concern with human freedom, then, leads to a focus on whether members of society have adequate opportunity to shape their lives rather than on whether absolute property rights are granted to members. We will shortly ask whether all Americans genuinely have adequate opportunity in this regard. But first I want to note that on the subject of opportunity, a concern to respect human *equality* in addition to human freedom will lead to a concern with more than just an adequate opportunity to shape one's life. In many contexts, after all, we often speak of the importance of *equal* opportunity. A dignity-based approach such as democratic liberalism implies that we are right to speak of this as important.

What exactly, though, do we mean when in political contexts we speak of the importance of "equal opportunity"? In fact, there is more than one way to define the ideal of equal opportunity; I will look at two such definitions. The first and least demanding definition of equal opportunity requires only that jobs be granted or denied to people on the basis of their qualifications, regardless of how they came by these qualifications. This familiar conception of equal opportunity—which we can refer to as *formal equality of opportunity*—rules out discrimination on the basis of race, ethnicity, sex, sexual orientation, religion, and so on. The conflict between this sort of discrimination and the ideal of equal citizenship is obvious. Martin Luther King Jr. perhaps described it most movingly in his famous "I Have a Dream" speech delivered at the Lincoln

Memorial on August 28, 1963, exactly one hundred years after President Abraham Lincoln's Emancipation Proclamation:

> One hundred years later, the life of the Negro is still sadly crippled by the manacles of segregation and the chains of discrimination. One hundred years later, the Negro lives on a lonely island of poverty in the midst of a vast ocean of material prosperity. One hundred years later, the Negro still languishes in the corners of American society and finds himself an exile in his own land.[35]

Discrimination, then, can reduce a person from an equal member of society into an internal exile ("an exile in his own land"). At best, discrimination treats another being as a nonentity whom it is fitting to confine to a "lonely island"—that is, to marginalize from society's mainstream. Worse yet, it can treat another being as a mere instrument, someone who exists to do the bottom-of-the-barrel, unwanted jobs in society, so that the people who really matter do not have to do them. Worst of all, it can signal that another being is to be regarded wholly with contempt and treated as a piece of refuse. As remarked earlier, such nonentitizing, instrumentalizing, and refusizing treatment is utterly inconsistent with respecting another being's dignity.[36]

The second definition of equality of opportunity goes beyond the first; following the philosopher John Rawls, we can refer to this conception as *fair equality of opportunity*.[37] In addition to requiring (like formal equality of opportunity) that job seekers be hired on the basis of their qualifications, fair equality of opportunity requires that job seekers have equal opportunity to obtain qualifications in the first place. In the contemporary United State this requirement is surely not met. Reports about the poor quality of inner-city schools compared with wealthy suburban schools are depressingly familiar, for example. Fixing this inequity will require equalizing the funding between urban and suburban schools. Unfortunately, one consequence of any such reform is that suburban dwellers will have to pay more in taxes than they currently do to keep their own schools at the same level of quality, since after such a reform they will share the costs along with inner-city residents of raising the latter's schools to suburban levels. This is unpleasant, of course, but it just reflects the fact that basic fairness, like other good things in life, is not free of charge. If we want a fair society in which all citizens are treated as equals, we need a level training field as much as a level playing field.[38] Thus the ideal of respect for dignity identifies fair equality of opportunity, rather than merely formal equality of opportunity, as the superior conception of equal opportunity.

We should not, however, deceive ourselves into thinking that improved education can by itself genuinely equalize the opportunity to acquire job qualifications. Differences in family cultures will remain, including the extent to which parents emphasize education; the amount they read to their children; the amount they are willing and able to help with homework; whether they can provide quiet areas for study; whether they teach their children good grammar and social skills; whether they are willing and able to take their children to museums, libraries, and other stimulating places; and so on.[39] These acts should not be required by law; among other reasons, to do so would violate the right to privacy mentioned above in section 4. Moreover, while the phenomena so far listed concern just education, family differences matter at the level of job competition too, of course. Family connections can help one get a job, and family wealth can pay for an elite college education, fund an unpaid summer internship to gain job skills, and provide much needed start-up funds for opening a business (or collateral for a business loan). In addition, individuals from rich families can take steep risks as young would-be entrepreneurs, secure in the confidence that they will not have to live in poverty should they fail.[40] And so on. While the economic advantages owing to family wealth can be blunted by public policy (say, with a more equitable distribution of wealth), those owing to family culture and connections cannot.

Economic opportunity, in short, will never truly be equal so long as the private family exists in some form, as it should. While we should strive to make opportunities more equal, we must at the same time recognize sensible limits to this ideal. But just as importantly, we should also avoid an opposite failing—namely, that of looking at differences in pay between people on different rungs of the economic ladder and wrongly reasoning that inasmuch as genuinely equal opportunity really does exist, each person is getting exactly the outcome he or she truly deserves. Judgments of desert require more nuance than this. The next section examines this subject.

7. Desert and Market Outcomes

Suppose we really did live in a society that was free of racial and other types of discrimination and that provided all its members with high-quality schools. Apart from the unequal opportunities stemming from differences in family wealth and family culture, could we say that in such a society all people get exactly the economic rewards they deserve to get, so that it would be morally objectionable to disturb whatever income distribution was produced by the workings of a capitalist marketplace (as happens, say, when taxes on the well-off help to fund health care, housing, and other forms of assistance for the poor)?

No. Far too many factors go toward determining your economic reward for there to be any simple correlation between this and your just deserts. For starters, much of your reward depends on luck. This luck takes several forms: simply being in the right place at the right time (say, a chance noticing of some job opening, or a chance meeting that leads to a useful business contact, etc.); or being born to the right family; or being born with genes that make one "gifted" in some way that the market values. Much of your economic compensation also depends on large-scale phenomena that are in no single individual's control: how scarce your skills are, what patterns of consumer taste prevail, what level of unemployment prevails in your society, where in the business cycle (the cycle between growth and recession) your society is, how competent the political and economic leaders of your society are, what collective bargaining agreements already exist, what natural resources are to be found in your society, what your society's level of technology is, and so on—for none of which you can individually take any credit. To better see this role that luck plays, consider that the average American today in 2005 commands vastly more resources than almost all Americans who lived in 1805, and vastly more than almost all Cambodians, say, in 2005. But is a typical American individual of today really personally more *deserving* of material comfort than nearly all Americans of 1805 and nearly all Cambodians of today? Surely not. This is *not* to say that no one deserves anything of what they earn. Rather, it is to say that applying a notion of desert to the economic realm is a tricky business and that we should thus avoid hasty conclusions to the effect that any and every interference with market outcomes involves taking away from people resources they are entitled to on grounds of desert.

A more reflective stance on economic desert would begin by asking what its basis is. Here we can usefully distinguish between objective criteria and subjective criteria. The claim that one deserves reward in proportion to one's *contribution to society* is an example of an objective criterion, whereas an example of a subjective criterion comes with the claim that one's deserts depend on the level of one's *efforts*—one's efforts, presumably, to be a productive member of society. This can usefully be thought of as a subjective version of the objective criterion of social contribution, since one's level of effort reflects the strength of one's desire to contribute to the economy.

In my view the choice between these objective and subjective criteria is not an easy one; in fact, I believe our common-sense moral beliefs attach importance to both criteria, even though they can conflict in many situations. Instead of trying to resolve this tension, I want to show that *neither* view of desert leads to a moral prohibition on any sort of interference with market outcomes. Start with an effort-based theory of desert. Clearly, one's financial rewards in an economic market do not depend merely on one's effort. I may try very hard to be a good mechanic, for instance, but if I do not succeed in my attempts to fix cars, I will eventually find myself with no customers; my (low) financial earnings will thus not match my (considerable) level of effort. On the other hand, if I am a wealthy investor (I own thousands of shares of Microsoft, say), I can earn a comfortable living just from the returns on my investments, with *no effort* on my part at all once the investment is made; my (high) financial earnings will thus not match my (nonexistent) level of effort. (I may spend some effort in monitoring my investments, of course—but if I am wealthy enough I can pay someone to do even this task for me.) Hence on an effort-based theory of desert it is simply not plausible to claim that in a perfectly free capitalist market each individual earns exactly what he or she deserves to earn; hence one cannot, on an effort-based theory of desert, oppose all interferences with market outcomes as either taking away from people money they deserve or giving to people money they do not deserve.

The theory of desert based on social contribution rather than effort is a more plausible foundation from which to argue that justice requires us to leave market outcomes alone. This argument runs as follows: The better one is able to produce goods that consumers desire, the more money one will typically earn; the producing of goods that consumers desire is a type of social contribution; hence, one's financial rewards in the free market match one's social contributions. This argument, however, is far from perfect, for the correlation between social contribution and financial reward is approximate at best. For example, porn king Larry Flynt, the founder of *Hustler* magazine, undoubtedly earns more in a year than, say, two hundred nurses combined earn, but does he really contribute more to the common good than two hundred nurses combined contribute, on any plausible way of measuring this? I doubt it. This is but one of many examples of a mismatch between reward and social contribution. Does a pro wrestler really contribute, say, forty times more than a superb daycare worker? What about a cigarette company executive versus a farmer? And so on.

Let us, however, temporarily waive these difficulties for the sake of argument. It is after all quite a challenge to know how best to measure a person's contribution to the common good, if not by market returns, and I lack the space here to confront this challenge. Even waiving the difficulties identified in the previous paragraph, however, we still do not yet have a contribution-based argument requiring us to leave market outcomes alone. For apart from self-employed individuals, the revenue from sales of a product or service accrue firstly to a *firm* rather than to the individual. What follows then from a contribution-based account of desert is that in a perfectly competitive market, the *group of people* constituting a firm collectively deserves the firm's revenue. This leaves as still to be addressed the question of how the group should divide its revenue amongst themselves.

On a contribution-based theory of desert, this question is answered by measuring each individual's contribution to the firm's production. But how should this be measured? One possible strategy suggests itself, namely, that an individual's contribution to the firm should be measured by whatever price his or her skills can command on an open labor market. However, this view assumes too rosy a picture of the way in which wages are determined. Consider for instance that your wages are influenced by the overall supply of people with your skills. If people with your skills suddenly become scarce, you will likely be able to demand a pay raise, even though your contribution to the firm's production remains what it always has been. In this case an increase in pay does not correspond to an increase in contribution. The flip side of this example is the case of someone with fairly common skills. Due to a large supply of these skills, such a person will command only a low wage, regardless of how essential his or her skills are to a firm's production. One example of this (out of many possible examples) is the case of janitors. They typically have low wages, despite the fact that janitors perform an essential service—without janitors other employees would have to work among piling-up trash and grime or do the job themselves and have far less time for their other tasks.[41] The same, moreover, can be said of any essential task, from stocking shelves to operating a cash register to loading trucks with freight.

A critic might try to defeat this point by saying that individuals could have avoided these lower-rung jobs had they merely "applied themselves" by studying harder in school. On this view, low wages are one's just deserts—punishment, of a sort—for past imprudence. This view, however, suffers from a number of flaws. First, we should remember our earlier observation that fair equality of opportunity to acquire qualifications or find a job does not yet prevail in our society and in fact never will, given differences in family culture and connections that no institution can fix. Not everybody has a fair go in life. Second, even if fair equality of opportunity *did* prevail, it is hardly the case that imprudent decisions made as a *teenager* truly make one deserving of lifelong low wages; such a "punishment" does not fit the "crime." Third, it may be that some people through bad genetic luck (a low innate intelligence, say) are simply not capable of performing more highly paid jobs. Finally, and most decisively, this view ignores the fact that such jobs as cleaning floors and emptying wastebaskets must be done by someone. If everyone were to gain a college degree, then this only means that someone with a college degree would end up cleaning floors, barring some technological breakthrough or some unprecedented system of sharing cleaning tasks among a wide pool of employees (which would in any case boost the wages associated with cleaning well above their current level). All of this reveals a mismatch between wages of workers at the bottom end and those workers' actual contributions to production.

A similar mismatch exists at the top end as well. Consider for instance the case of CEO pay compared to the pay of workers on the shop floor. According to *The Economist* (a right-of-center periodical), the top one hundred CEOs have an average annual compensation of $37.5 million each, over a thousand times the pay of the average worker.[42] This ratio represents a tremendous increase in less than a generation; thirty years ago, for example, the equivalent ratio was thirty-nine to one, with the top one hundred CEOs receiving an average of $1.3 million a year in pay.[43] In some individual cases, moreover, the ratio is now far higher than a thousand to one; for example, Ed Whitacre, the CEO of SBC Communications (a telecommunications company), was paid $83 million in 2001.[44] To put this into perspective, consider that a minimum-wage worker, earning $5.15 an hour and working forty hours a week with no vacations, would have to work 7,748 years to earn what Whitacre earned in this *single* year.

It is hard to believe the dramatic increase in CEO pay in recent years is entirely justified by a corresponding increase in CEOs' economic contributions. In fact, between 1990 and 2003 average CEO pay rose nearly two and a half times faster than did corporate profits.[45] Consider too that the pre-tax pay of chief executives in the United States is three times that of chief executives in similar-sized companies in Britain and four times those in France and Germany.[46] It is hard to believe that American CEOs are genuinely three to four times more productive than their European counterparts. A better explanation lies in the clubby nature in which many CEOs' pay is set. As Princeton economist Paul Krugman explains,

> The key reason executives are paid so much now is that they appoint the members of the corporate board that determines their compensation and control many of the perks that board members count on. So it's not the invisible hand of the market that leads to those monumental executive incomes; it's the invisible handshake in the boardroom.[47]

Since cronyism rather than productivity explains much of lavish CEO pay, there is an obvious mismatch between it and one's desert (understood as a function of one's contribution).

Beyond the issue of just CEO pay, we find a more general phenomenon of those people at the top of the American economic ladder reaping huge gains in comparison with the rest of workers. Between 1973 and 2000, for example, the average real income of the bottom 90 percent of American taxpayers actually fell by 7 percent, while the income of the top 1 percent of taxpayers rose by 148 percent.[48] Even within the top 1 percent bracket, gains were lopsided; the income of the top 0.1 percent rose by 343 percent, and the income of the top 0.01 percent rose 599 percent.[49] Indeed, the gains in income have been so strong at the high end that 94 percent of the growth in total income since 1973 has gone to the top 1 percent of taxpayers.[50] Clearly, America's increased prosperity in the last thirty years has not been shared with average workers.

Like generations past, however, American workers over the past thirty years have been doing their part to contribute to the economy; they thus deserve to share in the economy's increased prosperity. The important moral ideal at the root of this claim is one of *reciprocity*—those who contribute should benefit in kind. This moral ideal in fact follows from the deeper ideal of human equality, as I earlier interpreted this. For when exchanges in the labor market do not take place on a reciprocal footing, a morally objectionable asymmetry exists. One party is being unfairly taken advantage of—*exploited*, in a word—and thereby treated to some extent less like a person and more like a mere tool for another's purposes. Such instrumentalizing treatment, I earlier noted, is inconsistent with the ideal of human equality in its most defensible form.

In short, neither an effort-based nor a contribution-based account of desert supports the rather common view that the free market gives people exactly what they deserve. On this common but mistaken view, the free market is like a natural lake into which various gardeners dip their buckets; just as the amount of water withdrawn exactly matches the size of a person's bucket, on this view the free market's reward exactly matches the size of the contributions that a worker puts into it. The statistics cited above suggest a rather different metaphor. We should think of the economy not as a natural lake but instead as a man-made irrigation system, which like other man-made things is often in need of some adjustment: some workers toil in their modest garden patches while the irrigation system above drips meager amounts of water; meanwhile a leaky valve elsewhere in the system means others receive lavish amounts of water (and grow lavish gardens as a result).

Thinking of the economy as a man-made irrigation system is apt for another reason—a modern economy is certainly a man-made creation rather than a natural phenomenon. It is the creation of a dense network of very complex property and contract laws, together with a society's accountancy practices, prevailing styles of corporate governance, the actions of central banks (e.g., the Federal Reserve), regulatory schemes, and the functioning of police and the justice system, among other things—all of which take different forms in different capitalist countries. Given this complexity, it would be amazing indeed if any modern market economy succeeded in rewarding its participants exactly as they deserve.

Of course, even if man-made modern market economies often fail at the task of ensuring that people get what they deserve, it does not straightaway follow that any *nonmarket* institution—government, in particular—can succeed at this task. The centrally planned economies of the Soviet Union and its satellites, for example, were failures. But within a market framework, government may have a role to play in making the market more reciprocal than it otherwise would be. To advert to our earlier metaphor of an irrigation system, if some people are receiving inadequate amounts of water whereas others are overflowing in it then surely some plumbing is in order to remove the clogs and leaks that create inadequate and excessive flows. Government has a role to play here, most obviously in assisting those at the bottom of society, which I will shortly discuss. But government also has a less obvious role to play, in creating a framework within which individuals can do their own "plumbing."

What is needed for this are labor laws that create the space for various forms of employee organizations, so that employees have some significant say in their work conditions and pay. These organizations can take various forms, from traditional labor unions to "workers councils" to employee-owned firms. The first of these forms of organization (a labor union) is familiar to Americans; the remaining two forms are less familiar. Workers councils, common in Europe, do not collectively bargain as unions do over wages, hours, or benefits, but they do have significant legal rights to information and consultation with management on labor policies. In employee-owned firms, by contrast, workers have the same ultimate power over a firm's organization that shareholders in a traditional firm have; it is up to them how to use it.[51]

These forms of employee organization make it more likely that employee contributions receive the recognition they are due. But they are important for another reason as well, a reason that stems from the fact that an employer has a significant sort of power over employees, namely, the power to fire them. How significant this power is varies, of course; firing a teenager from a summer job is quite a different matter from firing a middle-aged parent whose family lives from paycheck to paycheck. In the large majority of cases, being fired is disruptive enough to one's life to make the threat alone an effective tool of employee control. The loss of earnings can be significant; finding a new job can sometimes be a lengthy process and often can require uprooting one's family and moving to a new location. At the extreme—say, if jobs are scarce and there is no safety net in the form of unemployment insurance, health insurance, etc.—the threat of being fired is a serious threat to one's health or even to one's life.

The power that employers have over employees is problematic from the point of view of respect for human dignity, much as the power of political rulers over the ruled is also problematic from this point of view. While in neither case is this power over others wholly eliminable, at the very least it should be made *accountable,* so that one does not live wholly at the mercy of those with power. Measures that can make employers' power accountable include health and safety laws that protect employees, laws defining sexual harassment (and other forms of harassment), and laws that facilitate the forms of employee organization mentioned above (unions, workers councils, employee-owned firms). In the latter case, laws can protect employees who are attempting to unionize against being dismissed, and they can require a firm to recognize a union once some significant threshold of employee support has been crossed.[52] Forms of encouragement, from tax breaks to regulatory relief, could also be given to firms that establish workers councils or are owned by their employees.

In short, rather than attempting to micromanage the economy in order to ensure each worker receives the treatment he or she deserves, it is better for the government to act for the most part *indirectly,* by facilitating forms of corporate governance in which employees have some significant say regarding their treatment. That said, there remains a direct role for government to play in aiding people at the bottom of the economic ladder. It is to this topic we turn in the next section.

8. A Dignified Minimum

One obvious form of support for people at the bottom is minimum-wage legislation. This acknowledges that full-time workers (who presumably are doing jobs that need doing by someone) deserve wages that enable them to live dignified lives. Wages below a decent minimum wage treat workers more like disposable instruments for others' needs than people with their own lives to live. The current level of $5.15—which totals to a mere $10,300 a year for a full-time worker who works fifty weeks a year—is surely too low. One obstacle in the way of raising the minimum wage is the widespread belief that this would increase unemployment. Recent research by the economists Alan Krueger and David Card, however, has cast serious doubt on this claim. In a "controlled experiment" of sorts, Krueger and Card compared the effect on low-wage employment of a raise

in New Jersey's minimum-wage laws with similar employment a few miles away in Pennsylvania (a state that had not
recently raised its minimum wage); there was little discernible
difference in unemployment rates.[53] Moreover, there are other
ways apart from minimum-wage laws by which to raise the
wages of low-end workers. The current Earned Income Tax
Credit, for instance, is a refundable tax credit that significantly
boosts the income of working families in the United States. (In
this scheme low-income workers receive a credit to apply
against their taxes; they then receive a check for any part of
their credit that is unused once their taxes are paid. This can
increase a low-income family's earnings by several thousand
dollars a year, thereby reducing poverty. In 1999, for instance,
the Earned Income Tax Credit lifted 4.7 million working families above the poverty line.)[54]

Another direct way for government to repair some of the
shortcomings of the market is to maintain a social safety net, in
the form of unemployment insurance, social security, and measures to ensure that health insurance is affordable. In addition
to these benefits (which poor and nonpoor alike receive), there
should be maintenance income for those in poverty. In fact,
even those who never find themselves in need of this safety net
benefit from it. Partly this benefit consists in *peace of mind* that
one will not find oneself in abject destitution. But that is not the
whole of the benefit; the social safety net also benefits even
those who never receive its payments inasmuch as it dulls the
edge of employer power over employees. Since it cushions the
blow one would receive in the event of losing one's job, the social safety net makes an employer's threat of firing less fear-
some and thereby helps to keep his or her power over others
within reasonable bounds. (In this regard, one current hole in
the American safety net concerns health care. Around forty-
five million Americans lack health insurance, and those who
do have it usually receive it through their employers.[55] Receiving health care through an employer is clearly far from ideal,
however, inasmuch as this can tie a person to his or her current

job, reducing his or her employment options and thereby increasing an employer's threat power.)[56]

That said, one of the most obvious functions of the social safety net is that of helping those people at the bottom of the economic ladder. This function is necessary in order to make real the ideal of equal citizenship discussed earlier, which rules out citizens having to live as "internal exiles" in their own land, marginalized from society's mainstream. Deep poverty conflicts with this ideal, for it rules out much of what middle-class citizens take for granted: owning one's own home, having a reliable car, attending sporting events, going away on vacation, providing music lessons (or other extras) for one's children, belonging to a gym, and so on. An important role of the social safety net lies in dismantling the poverty traps that can deny individuals effective access to these mainstream experiences and others.

Of course, whether poor individuals are to a significant extent trapped in poverty or rather are failing to avail themselves of the opportunities they already possess is a controversial question that makes debates over the welfare provisions of the social safety net especially heated. A full explanation of the causes of poverty is clearly beyond the scope of this short essay. Let me instead simply say that while the causes of poverty are complex, many citizens' views on poverty unfortunately consist of little more than stereotypes. For instance, consider the popular image of poor people as made up mainly of "welfare queens"—the image of nonworking African-American women who live in ghettos supporting their out-of-wedlock children on government checks year after year. In fact, 51 percent of the poor are (non-Hispanic) *white,* compared to 25 percent who are black; 37 percent live in suburbs; 66 percent of the poor do not live in female-headed families; and among poor family heads (male and female), 60 percent are employed, with 23 percent of poor family heads working at least fifty weeks a year, full-time.[57] Over the period 1979–1991, moreover, fully one-third of Americans were poor for at least one year, but only 5 percent were poor for ten years or more.[58] This variety is indeed what one should expect, given the large number of poor people in America—35.8 million people in 2003, according to the most recent data at the time of writing, equivalent to 12.5 percent of all Americans (up from 12.2 percent in 2002).[59]

Hence the poor comprise more kinds of people than popular belief supposes. The same is surely true of the causes of poverty. Yes, a significant chunk of poverty is undoubtedly due to imprudent decisions made on the part of individuals. But not all of it is. As just noted, many of the poor are working hard, struggling to make ends meet. In addition, many are unemployable on account of old age or severe disability. Limitations on opportunities explain a significant amount of poverty as well. We have already noted the inequalities in opportunity that exist in public education and in family cultures and connections. Moreover, even apart from these inequalities, economic opportunity itself is not unlimited; in particular, it is not the case that everyone who wants a job can easily find one. This is obvious in a recession, when the unemployment rate is high. But involuntary unemployment is always present to some extent, owing to the way the economy is managed by the Federal Reserve. If the unemployment rate dips too "low"—below what economists call the "non-accelerating inflation rate of unemployment" (NAIRU)—then the Federal Reserve will raise interest rates to slow down the economy (the economy will slow, because higher interest rates mean less business investment in new projects); this deceleration in turn will bring the unemployment rate back up (fewer new business projects means less need for employees).[60] This is not a nefarious plan on the part of the Federal Reserve; its goal is to prevent runaway inflation (which can be sparked by an extremely tight labor market), and runaway inflation is indeed worth avoiding, even at the cost of some unemployment.[61] But the Fed's policy does mean there will always be a significant number of people who at any given moment are unable to find a job through no fault of their own.

Acknowledging these points is compatible with also acknowledging that some abuse of the welfare system does exist. The right to public assistance is not a boundless right,
and abuse is a matter of serious concern. It is important to
note, however, that the existence of some amount of abuse
does not straightaway entail that the entire welfare system
should be scrapped, any more than the existence of some
speeding entails that we should do away with the highway
system. For to scrap the entire welfare system would be to
leave some citizens trapped in destitution. In short, any
given society here has a choice between (1) deciding to help
those who are poor, at the cost of tolerating some abuse of
the system; or (2) deciding to tolerate no abuse whatsoever,
at the cost of leaving the non-abusing majority of the poor in
humiliating conditions. Surely choice (1) is preferable, for
while the cost of welfare abuse pinches an individual tax-
payer only slightly (since the total cost is spread among millions of similar taxpayers), the cost of being trapped in
poverty pinches a poor individual hard enough to devastate
his or her life.

All the same, a society is within its rights to try to reduce
the level of abuse it must tolerate. The first step is to understand exactly what behavior is abuse and what is not. This
should be understood with reference to the ideal of reciprocity. It is not abuse for the elderly and severely disabled to receive support without working, for example; because they
are not employable, their nonwork does not amount to treating their fellow citizens as mere instruments in support of
their own purposes.[62] However, able-bodied citizens of working age who draw support while not seeking work (or training for it) instrumentalize their fellow citizens, provided that
non-humiliating work opportunities do in fact exist for them.
Such behavior is a departure from the ideal of reciprocity. For
this reason it is compatible with respect for human dignity to
require those who receive public assistance to work, when
possible.

Building a work requirement into a system of public assistance must be done right, however. For example, at least two challenges arise when those who receive public assistance are single parents caring for dependent children. To see the first such challenge, note that child rearing is in general socially productive labor, although it is not paid; society after all needs to be replenished with new generations. In a sense, then, single parents on public assistance are in fact already working. I do not think, however, that this fact by itself ought entirely to exempt single parents from a work requirement. A society can conceivably acknowledge in general the social contributions of parents and at the same time judge that particular forms of parenting—namely, single parenting in conditions of poverty and unemployment—are inauspicious enough not to warrant subsidizing. A second challenge that arises with requiring single parents to work concerns the cost of childcare. Reliable childcare is expensive, and the low-wage jobs for which welfare mothers are eligible often do not pay enough to make it affordable. For this reason work requirements need to be accompanied by vouchers or refundable tax credits that make childcare accessible to low-income workers. If this is not done, it is innocent children who will pay the price up front, and society who will pay the price later when these children become adults. (Indeed, there are independent reasons to provide high-quality day care for poor children; a number of recent studies suggest that it can in fact pay for itself by reducing rates of juvenile delinquency and crime later on, as well as by raising rates of college attendance.)[63]

Whatever the form a work requirement takes, it should not be seen as a form of punishment for poverty, as it was in the poorhouses of the past. Rather, it is simply an acknowledgment that the ideal of reciprocity imposes obligations on all persons—on the well-off, not to treat fellow citizens as nonentities who can be abandoned to suffer in degrading conditions; and on the poor, not to exploit the good will of their fellow citizens.[64] Indeed, this ideal of reciprocity ought also to lead us to adjust somewhat our understanding of the goal of public assistance, which is usually described as enabling individuals to become "self-supporting." This is a laudable goal, but as described it is misleading, for *no* person apart from a bona fide Robinson Crusoe–type is genuinely self-sufficient. Instead, we are all mutually dependent on each other's playing his or her part in the economy at large, which is in truth a system of joint production that is not the making of any single individual.[65] The goal of welfare and other provisions of the social safety net is best described not as making current welfare recipients "self-sufficient" but instead as moving them into a more balanced relation of reciprocity with their fellow citizens. But by the same token, the goal is also to move well-off citizens into a more balanced relation of reciprocity with less well-off citizens, by requiring them to acknowledge that all citizens who do their part in a system of joint production are at a minimum entitled to a life of dignity.

9. Conclusion

Throughout this essay I have defended an understanding of human dignity in terms of the capability for responsible choice, together with an ideal of respect for human dignity thus understood—an ideal that establishes very strong presumptions against diminishing, obscuring, or insulting human dignity. This has helped illuminate such fundamental values as freedom and equality. It has also led to an endorsement of democratic liberalism, yielding plausible conclusions as regards the structure of individual rights, democracy, and the economy. A glance back at the *wergild* system of medieval times, which by law punished the murder of a prince differently from the murder of a peasant, shows how far we have traveled down the path of respecting dignity, toward democratic liberalism. Now we have the challenge of traveling the rest of the way together.

Notes

1. Thomas Aquinas, *Summa Theologica*, Prima Secundae, q. 87, a. 4, arg. 2. Quoted in Marilyn McCord Adams, "Hell and the God of Justice," *Religious Studies* 11 (1979): 442.

2. Adams, "Hell and the God of Justice," 442. *Wergild* literally means "manprice" in Anglo-Saxon (www.en.wikipedia.org/wiki/Wergild).

3. William James, *Essays in Pragmatism* (New York: Hafner, 1948), 68.

4. In focusing specifically on *human* dignity, I do not mean to suggest that all talk of dignity is out of place as regards nonhuman animals. For excellent discussion of this issue, see Martha Nussbaum, *Frontiers of Justice: Disability, Nationality, Species Membership* (Cambridge, Mass.: Harvard University Press, 2005), chap. 6.

5. The preamble to the United Nations' Universal Declaration of Human Rights (1948), for instance, begins, "Whereas recognition of the *inherent dignity* and of equal and inalienable rights of all members of the human family is the foundation of freedom, justice, and peace in the world" [emphasis added]. Available at www.un.org/Overview/rights.html.

6. I speak of observing a *strong presumption* against impairing, constraining, and ignoring the capacity for responsible choice, rather than an *absolute prohibition* against these, because the theory I will defend is not an absolutist theory. We may face tragic choices in which, say, constraining a person is necessary to prevent even graver indignities to others. I will have more to say about this later in section 3.

7. It is not necessarily destroyed altogether, for as I observed in note 4, there may be other forms of dignity besides the characteristic human sort located in the capacity for responsible choice.

8. To be sure, this account of human equality does not grant equal status to absolutely every living being with human DNA. Profoundly retarded individuals and young children do not make the cut, for instance. This by itself is not an objection to my proposed foundation for moral equality, however, since to my knowledge no one proposes treating young children or the profoundly retarded—someone who understands no language of any kind, for instance—exactly the same as citizens generally (e.g., granting them the right to vote). This does not imply, however, that these human beings have *no* rights of any kind. Children's status as responsible beings in training will give them certain rights. Profoundly retarded people's status as bearers of tragic misfortune will morally rule out subjecting them to further indignities beyond what they already suffer by nature; one should not kick people who are already down. Beyond these merely suggestive remarks, however, in the short space I have here I will not address further the difficult question of what

rights incompetents possess. For more discussion on the disabled, see Martha Nussbaum, *Frontiers of Justice*, chaps. 2 and 3.

9. Immanuel Kant, *Groundwork of the Metaphysic of Morals*, trans. H. J. Paton (New York: Harper and Row, 1964), 96.

10. Aristotle, *The Politics and the Constitution of Athens*, rev. student ed., trans. Benjamin Jowett, ed. Stephen Everson (Cambridge, U.K.: Cambridge University Press, 1996), 1253a3.

11. For information and references on feral children, see the material at www.feralchildren.com.

12. Playing a sport is a type of cooperative activity, despite the presence of competition. For to play a sport genuinely is to commit oneself, to a significant extent, to play by the rules of the sport. (Think of the ideal of good sportsmanship, for example). Someone who sees no intrinsic reason not to cheat is not playing a sport; rather, he is treating it as something like a ritual that is to be exploited (rather than participated in) for his own ends. In analogous fashion, the presence of economic competition does not fundamentally alter the cooperative aspect of society. If economic competition degenerates into a no-holds-barred struggle to destroy others, *society* has disappeared and been replaced by something akin to a ritualized form of warfare.

13. This has not, however, stopped some philosophers (e.g., John Locke) from claiming that appearances are deceiving, that in fact all members of society *do* consent—tacitly consent—to its rules. For my criticism of this claim, see chapter 2, section 3 of this book.

14. John Rawls, *Political Liberalism* (New York: Columbia University Press, 1993), 137.

15. For further astute discussion of this contrast, and of the idea of shaping a life, see Richard Norman, *Ethics, Killing, and War* (Cambridge, U.K.: Cambridge University Press, 1995), chap. 2.

16. I believe that the right to freedom of religion—a right of fundamental importance—is in fact entailed by the rights to freedom of expression, association, and conscience. Thus there is no need to list it separately. If I am wrong about this, then of course freedom of religion should be added to the list alongside these other freedoms. For further discussion of this matter, see Andrew Altman, "Freedom of Speech and Religion," in *The Oxford Handbook of Practical Ethics*, ed. Hugh Lafollette (Oxford, U.K.: Oxford University Press, 2004), 358–86.

17. This point is made in Joshua Cohen's admirable article, "Freedom of Expression," *Philosophy and Public Affairs* 22 (1993): 207–63.

18. Moreover, if in a given society citizens are *not* in general competent to lead their lives, one must ask whether this is remediable through improvements in the education system, rather than inherent in the nature of things. I believe our modern experience with liberal democracy shows that with a good education citizens in general can achieve such competency.

19. Cf. the words of the French philosopher Helvétius: "To limit the press is to insult a nation; to prohibit reading of certain books is to declare the inhabitants to be either fools or slaves" (Claude Adrien Helvétius, *De L'Homme* [London: Thoemmes, 1999], vol. 1, sec. 4). The main idea of this passage is surely correct, though as I note in what follows, some narrowly defined limits to freedom of expression are necessary.

20. *Brandenburg v. Ohio* (1969), 395 U.S. 444.

21. *New York Times Co. v. Sullivan* (1964), 376 U.S. 254

22. For some innovative suggestions along these lines, see Bruce A. Ackerman and James F. Fishkin, *Deliberation Day* (New Haven, Conn.: Yale University Press, 2004).

23. For useful information on these various ways (and their pros and cons), see the website of the Center for Voting and Democracy at www.fairvote.org.

24. These statistics are available at the website of the Center for Responsive Politics (www. opensecrets.org/bigpicture; click on links labeled "The Price of Admission" and "Different Races, Different Costs").

25. URL www.opensecrets.org/pressreleases/Post-Election2000.htm.

26. URL www.opensecrets.org/bigpicture.

27. URL www.opensecrets.org/pressreleases/Post-Election2000.htm.

28. URL www.opensecrets.org/presidential/index.asp. .

29. For one such example involving the company Enron and House majority leader Tom DeLay, see Paul Krugman, "Machine At Work," *New York Times*, July 13, 2004. For an in-depth study of an earlier example, see Jeffrey H. Birnbaum and Alan S. Murray, *Showdown at Gucci Gulch: Lawmakers, Lobbyists, and the Unlikely Triumph of Tax Reform* (New York: Vintage Books, 1988).

30. Public Campaign, "The Road to Clean Elections," (www.publicampaign.org/publications/trtce/TheRoadToCleanElections.pdf).

31. Clean Elections Institute, Inc., "2002 Success of Clean Elections" (www.azclean.org/documents/2002SuccessStats.doc).

32. Clean Elections Institute, Inc., "2002 Success of Clean Elections."

33. Clean Elections Institute, Inc., "2002 Success of Clean Elections."

34. Clean Elections Institute, Inc., "The Road to Victory" (www .azclean.org/documents/ 2002RoadtoVictory-Final.pdf). The money comes from fees on lobbyists who represent for-profit activities and from a ten percent surcharge on civil and criminal fines (Public Campaign, "The Road to Clean Elections").

35. Martin Luther King, Jr., "I Have a Dream," in *The Moral Life*, 2nd ed., ed. Louis Pojman (Oxford, U.K.: Oxford University Press, 2003), 649.

36. Race relations have improved significantly since the time of King's speech, thanks in large measure to the Civil Rights Movement's victories in the form of the 1964 Civil Rights Act and 1965 Voting Rights Act. We still have a significant way to go before racial discrimination is eliminated, however. For evidence of continued discrimination, see chapter 6, section 3 of this book.

37. John Rawls, *A Theory of Justice*, rev. ed. (Cambridge, Mass.: Harvard University Press, 1999), 63.

38. For valuable suggestions as to how to spend the extra money raised for failing schools, see Matthew Miller, *The Two Percent Solution: Fixing America's Problems in Ways Liberals and Conservatives Can Love* (New York: Public Affairs, 2003), chap. 6.

39. Cf. Richard Rothstein, *Class and Schools* (Washington, D.C.: Economic Policy Institute, 2004).

40. This point is made in Brian Barry, *Why Social Justice Matters* (Cambridge, U.K.: Polity, 2005), 194.

41. Cf. Elizabeth S. Anderson, "What Is the Point of Equality?" *Ethics* 109 (1999): 322. My defense of democratic liberalism is heavily indebted to this article.

42. "Special Report: Ever higher society, ever harder to ascend—Meritocracy in America," *The Economist*, January 1, 2005, 22–25. This article also reports that social mobility (i.e., individuals' likelihood of moving up the class ladder) has *declined* in the United States since the 1970s, to point where the United States now has less social mobility than many other countries, such as Germany, Sweden, Finland, and Canada. This decline in mobility has begun to worry even conservative commentators; see for instance David Brooks, "The Sticky Ladder," *New York Times*, January 1, 2005.

43. "Special Report," *The Economist*, 24. This figure is adjusted for inflation.

44. Matthew Boyle, "When Will They Stop?" *Fortune*, May 3, 2004, 123.

45. Robert Trigaux, "Executive Compensation Rises through Lavish to Absurd," *St. Petersburg Times*, April 26, 2004 (www.sptimes.com/2004/04/26/Columns/Executive_compensatio.shtml). For further data see the summary at www.faireconomy.org/press/2004/CEOPayRatio_pr.html and Lucian Bebchuk and Jesse Fried, *Pay without Performance: The Unfulfilled Promise of Executive Compensation* (Cambridge, Mass.: Harvard University Press, 2004).

46. Alan B. Krueger, "When It Comes to Income Inequality, More Than Just Market Forces Are at Work," *New York Times*, April 4, 2002.

47. Paul Krugman, "For Richer," *New York Times Magazine*, October 20, 2002, 66. See Derek Bok, *The Cost of Talent: How Executives and Professionals Are Paid and How It Affects America* (New York: Free Press, 2002) for an extended study of CEO pay.

48. Paul Krugman, "The Death of Horatio Alger," *The Nation*, January 5, 2004 (www.thenation.com/doc.mhtml?i=20040105&s=krugman).

49. Krugman, "The Death of Horatio Alger."

50. Krueger, "When It Comes to Income Inequality."

51. For a sophisticated defense of worker-owned firms, see Samuel Bowles and Herbert Gintis, "A Political and Economic Case for the Democratic Enterprise," *Economics and Philosophy* 9 (1993): 75–100.

52. Laws like this already exist in the United States, but the monetary sanctions levied against firms who fire union-seeking employees are so minimal that many businesses break these laws with little hesitation and treat the fines as just another routine cost of business. Another problem is firms' ability to delay recognition of a union for years (sometimes as much as ten years) owing to a ridiculously slow recognition process overseen by the National Labor Relations Board. For details see Human Rights Watch, *Unfair Advantage: Workers' Freedom of Association in the United States under International Human Rights Standards* (2000), available online at www.hrw.org/reports/2000/uslabor. For valuable suggestions as to how to improve U.S. labor laws, see Richard Freeman, "Lessons for the United States," in *Working under Different Rules,* ed. Richard Freeman, 223–39 (New York: Russell Sage Foundation, 1994). These problems help explain the extraordinary decline in unionization rates in the United States, to the point where by 2003 under 9 percent of the private sector was unionized, *less than half* the unionization rate of every other industrial democracy (www.aflcio/ecouncil/ec02262003b.cfm). This is surely part of the reason that average wages have fallen in the United States over the past two decades, while in the same period they have *risen* in every other OECD country—that is, every other major developed country. (See Richard Freeman, "The New Inequality in the United States," in *Growing Apart: The Causes and Consequences of the Global Wage Inequality,* eds. Albert Fishlow and Karen Parker [New York: Council on Foreign Relations Press, 1999], 29).

53. David Card and Alan B. Krueger, *Myth and Measurement: The New Economics of the Minimum Wage* (Princeton, N.J.: Princeton University, 1995). Other natural experiments are also examined in this book. See also the symposium on the book in *Industrial and Labor Relations Review* 48:4 (1995). For a concise summary of the shift in thinking among many economists regarding the minimum wage, see Thomas Palley, "Building Prosperity from the Bottom Up," *Challenge* 41 (1998): 59–72.

54. Center on Budget and Policy Priorities, "Facts about the Earned Income Credit: Tax Time Can Pay for Working Families" (2004), 21, citing the U.S. Census Bureau's Current Population Survey; available online at www.cbpp.org/eic2004/eic04-factbook.pdf.

55. Associated Press, "Ranks of Poverty and Uninsured Rose in 2003, Census Reports," *New York Times,* August 26, 2004 (www.nytimes.com). Forty-five million Americans constitute 15.6 percent of the population. This is an increase from the 15.2 percent of Americans who lacked health insurance in 2002.

56. For a helpful overview of America's employer-based health insurance, see Uwe E. Reinhardt, "Employer-Based Health Insurance: A Balance Sheet," *Health Affairs* 18 (1999): 124–33. See Miller, *The Two Percent Solution,*

chap. 5, for a discussion of what is probably the most feasible option in the American context for fixing this hole in the safety net (namely, "community rated" private insurance plus a requirement that all citizens purchase health insurance, with the poor assisted by public subsidies). For examples of health systems from other countries, which can serve as useful comparisons, see Laurene Graig, *Health of Nations: An International Perspective on U.S. Health Care Reform* (Washington, D.C.: Congressional Quarterly Books, 1999). Finally, for insightful philosophical reflection on health care, see Ronald Dworkin, *Sovereign Virtue: The Theory and Practice of Equality* (Cambridge, Mass.: Harvard University Press, 2000), chap. 8.

57. Mary Jo Bane and Lawrence M. Mead, *Lifting Up the Poor: A Dialogue on Religion, Poverty and Welfare* (Washington, D.C.: Brookings Institution Press, 2003), 59. The figures are for the year 2001 and come from the U.S. Census Bureau's March 2002 Annual Demographic Supplement, tables 2–4. The Census Bureau's threshold for poverty was $18,104/year for a family of four in 2001. One reason for popular misconceptions about the poor lies with media images that disproportionately display poverty as a black phenomenon. For a sophisticated media critique, see Martin Gilens, *Why Americans Hate Welfare: Race, Media, and the Politics of Antipoverty Policy* (Chicago: University of Chicago Press, 2000). For full-length studies of the working poor, see Katherine S. Newman, *No Shame in My Game: The Working Poor of the Inner City* (New York: Vintage Books, 2000) and David K. Shipler, *The Working Poor: Invisible in America* (New York: Knopf, 2004).

58. Bane and Mead, *Lifting Up the Poor*, 58.

59. Associated Press, "Ranks of Poverty and Uninsured Rose."

60. Paul Krugman, "Labor Pains," *New York Times Magazine*, May 24, 1999, 24–26.

61. A significant number of economists, however, believe the importance of NAIRU has been overrated and that the Federal Reserve could do more to lower unemployment without creating runaway inflation. See for example James K. Galbraith, *Created Unequal: The Crisis in American Pay* (Chicago: University of Chicago Press, 2000); Thomas I. Palley, *Plenty of Nothing: The Downsizing of the American Dream and the Case for Structural Keynesianism* (Princeton, N.J.: Princeton University Press, 2000); and George A. Akerlof, "Behavioral Macroeconomics and Macroeconomic Behavior," *American Economic Review* 92 (2002), 411–33. For a variety of viewpoints, see the symposium on NAIRU in the *Journal of Economic Perspectives* 11:1 (1997).

62. In saying that the seriously disabled are not employable, I have in mind primarily those with very serious mental disabilities. A person in a wheelchair is employable, of course, provided he or she can reach the workplace. Considerations of dignity point to the need for laws requiring businesses to make reasonable accommodations for the physically disabled, so

that they too can participate in work. Cf. Nussbaum, *Frontiers of Justice,* chaps. 2 and 3.

63. For a summary of recent studies see Alan B. Krueger, "Inequality, Too Much of a Good Thing" (Unpublished manuscript), available online at www.irs.princeton.edu/pubs/pdfs/inequality4.pdf). See also the Committee for Economic Development's 2002 report, "Preschool for All: Investing in a Productive and Just Society" (www.ced.org/docs/report/report _preschool.pdf).

64. This point bears on an assessment of the Personal Responsibility and Work Opportunity Reconciliation Act of 1996 (PRWORA), by which the U.S. Congress instituted work requirements as a condition of welfare receipt. On the whole, the framework I am employing supports this reform, though I think *much* less attention was paid to crucial issues of childcare and job training than was necessary. The most successful systems of welfare in America, such as the Minnesota Family Investment Program, pay a great deal of attention to these issues. For details, see Dave Hage, *Reforming Welfare by Rewarding Work: One State's Successful Experiment* (Minneapolis: University of Minnesota Press, 2004). I am skeptical, moreover, of one other significant element of PRWORA, namely, its time limits, which restrict federal welfare receipt to a total of five years over the course of a single lifetime. I know of no a priori guarantee that misfortune never totals to longer than five years for any individual.

65. I take the term "system of joint production" from Anderson, "What Is the Point of Equality?" 321.

5

The Follies of Democratic "Liberalism"

Tibor R. Machan

One of the ways contemporary philosophers go about supporting various ethical and political ideas and ideals is by considering what we all supposedly take to be intuitively right and good. Professor Duncan gives us a good example when he quotes William James, regarding "the 'emotion' [of] respect, namely, for the dignity of that 'certain lost soul' whose torture would guarantee the happiness of millions" (p. 81). That feeling is supposed to be a decisive indicator of what we all ought to value. Duncan shares this methodology with several other twentieth-century moral and political philosophers, including the most famous of them, John Rawls, who invokes intuitions as part of his foundation for his ethical and political reflections and recommendations in *A Theory of Justice*.[1]

Yet, as Rawls himself came to realize in his later book *Political Liberalism*,[2] the intuitions on which his own ideal of justice relies are far from universal among human beings. Rawls noted in his later work that the principles he identifies as crucial to a just society are mostly applicable in the context of Western political history. He could have gone farther and noted that even in the West, there are many competing intuitions. The writer W. Somerset Maugham put it well when he noted that "intuition [is] a subject upon which certain philosophers have reared an imposing edifice of surmise, but which seems to me to offer as insecure a foundation for any structure more substantial than a Castle in Spain as a ping pong ball wavering on a jet of water in a shooting gallery."[3] Consider the following as support for what Maugham is noting:

> To us today the revelation of the legal murders and cruelties connected with the trial of children are revolting. We have become so habituated to the kindly and even anxious atmosphere of the Children's Courts, that it is hard to believe that the full ceremonial, the dread ordeal, of the Assize Courts could have been brought into use against little children of seven years and upwards—judges uttering their cruel legal platitudes; the chaplain sitting by assenting; the Sheriff in his impressive uniform; ladies coming to the Court to be entertained by such a sight—the spectacle of a terrified little child about to receive the death sentence which the verdict of 12 men, probably fathers of families themselves, had given the judge power to pass.[4]

Many other practices and beliefs, held equally firmly and "naturally," could be cited to illustrate the problem with resting decisive moral and political ideas and ideals on intuitions or feelings. In Duncan's analysis the belief in the fundamental value of the sort of equality he champions is made to rest on intuitions, but that is not a good enough reason for us to accept what he is advocating.

As I stress in my own opening essay, however, there is a version of egalitarianism that does deserve serious support; it rests not on intuition but on the facts that human nature is ubiquitous (other than in crucially incapacitated persons) and that from it certain basic principles are derivable, principles that then equally apply to all. This is the natural-rights position that I find most convincing, one that is associated with John Locke and other natural law/natural rights defenders of classical liberalism and libertarianism. It is, of course, an egalitarianism that is limited to equal respect for the human dignity of each person, a dignity that involves the distinctive capacity to be, in adulthood, a moral agent. It is this naturalist, rather than intuition based, conception of human dignity that supports the political imperative to respect the rights of all human beings and the ethical imperative to establish a legal order for the protection of those rights.[5]

In the matter of our distinctive (enough) human nature, which renders us but not other animals moral agents, Duncan and I are not so far apart.[6] Duncan, however, seems to develop his democratic liberal politics more along lines we learn from Martha Nussbaum, also a neo-Aristotelian naturalist, who supports an extensive welfare state rather than the libertarian polity I consider just and proper.[7] Duncan says, accordingly, "The most devastating way one can fail to respect another person's dignity is by failing to recognize any presumption against *impairing* that person's capacity for responsible choice" (p. 83). Doing so, however, is not confined to violations of that person's negative rights—to, say, life, liberty, property, and so forth—but extends to failing to enable the person to develop in such a way that responsible choice is likely to emerge in his or her life. The following makes clear how Duncan arrives at his robust egalitarian politics from a conception of human nature that is rather similar to that which I have associated with normative classical liberalism:

> I propose we understand society as a system of cooperation by which members gain in their ability to complete the fundamental tasks of living. Certainly, compared to a solitary existence, life in society better enables us to feed, clothe, shelter, and protect ourselves from nature's threats. The enablement that social cooperation makes possible need not be limited to enabling us in meeting our basic needs, however. (pp. 87–88).[8]

Once one understands society as "a system of cooperation," one needs to ask for what purpose such a system would be most appropriate and what terms of cooperation may be required of all members of society.

There is a problem, just for starters, with the concept "cooperation," namely, that its meaning includes the idea of the *voluntary mutual interaction* of human beings. Such interaction is itself open to moral assessment. One can, after all, cooperate in carrying out evil deeds.[9] What is it, however, that the cooperation that supposedly gives rise to society aims at—or should aim at? This is crucial, because the answer will determine some of the constitutive features of a just society. In other words, not any society, even if voluntarily established, may be just.

Furthermore, there are societies that are not established voluntarily, at least if we go by ordinary usage. North Korea, the Third Reich, Cuba, and apartheid-ridden South Africa were or are all societies, yet they are by no means cooperative human associations. Aristotle's polis was by no means a cooperative association of human beings.[10]

But let us not get bogged down here. There are more important matters to consider in Duncan's discussion.[11] I want instead to turn to Duncan's support for democracy, a support that may arguably be taken as *illiberal*, in the sense spelled out by Fareed Zakaria in his recent book *The Future of Freedom*.[12] Duncan tells us this to start with, without realizing that he is ignoring the most important problem with democracy, namely, its proneness to be illiberal.

> One important question concerns whether to have a *direct* democracy (in which citizens themselves propose and vote on laws) or a *representative* democracy (in which elected offices perform these functions). To a large extent this question is settled by pragmatic considerations (direct democracies are better suited to small city-states than to today's large nation-states), but a dignity-based case is not wholly silent here. I do not believe that the demands of dignity *require* direct democracy, for to say that citizens are competent beings capable of responsible choice is not to say they are all competent to judge the various issues requiring political atten-

tion, from taxes to defense to education to the environment, and so on. A representative democracy instead, and more accurately, presumes citizens are first and foremost competent to choose leaders who are themselves competent at judging these issues. This is not to say that the ideal of direct democracy has no relevance, however. Since in fact many private citizens do have competent knowledge of a variety of issues, especially those that directly implicate their interests, a representative democracy should also create significant space for citizen input into its deliberative practices (via open hearings and other public forums, say) (p. 95).

This entire passage and what follows it fail to raise a most important question, namely, the *proper scope* of either direct or representative democracy. The issue is well known by reference to the shopworn example of the lynch mob. It is directly democratic, if it involves everyone in a given community, or representatively democratic, if the leaders step forward to carry out the will of the people (which is not, of course, Rousseau's *general will* by a long shot).

The libertarian, in contrast, approaches democracy much more skeptically. Although to a great many people around the globe democracy is nearly synonymous with liberty—they think when they say "a democratic country" that they are referring to one that is a free country—this is not at all assured. Yes, there is something to the common impression, because in a free country, sure enough, everyone is free, among other things, *to vote*, to take part in the political process.[13] When some people (other than criminals) do not have this aspect of the right to liberty respected and protected, the country is clearly not sufficiently free.

But is democracy enough for a country to be free? No. A country can even lose its freedom democratically, as when the majority, once it has gained power, curtails the freedom of the minority. Indeed, one important way to explain and understand the rise of Hitler is that in the Weimar Republic the majority voted him into power and thus abolished not only freedom but democracy.

What then is the right relationship between democracy and liberty? I am, of course, talking about the kind of liberty that means not violating the basic rights of anyone. (There is freedom or liberty of the kind that has nothing to do with rights but concerns so enabling one that he or she can do things. That kind of freedom is secured through productivity, by providing oneself—or, as in welfare states, being provided with by others—with various resources that make it possible to do things.) Can democracy even exist as a procedure in a society that is fully committed to liberty or, rather, to the respect and protection of the right to do what one wants?

Actually, despite the fact that a bloated democracy is incompatible with full liberty for all, individual liberty and democracy are compatible, provided democracy is applied within limits. The best-known example of such limits is made evident in the case of the lynch mob. Since the lynch mob, though democratic, fails to adhere to certain rules, it is actually tyrannical. The majority proceeds to impose measures that violate individual rights (to, say, a justly conducted trial, one that observes due[!] process). This example can help us see how democracy requires limits in order to be compatible with liberty.

But what is there left for the democratic process to address if it must be limited by certain rules? Two matters are directly at issue here.

For a free country to be established successfully, it needs majority support. This is a matter of power. Freedom cannot be secured unless there is plenty of power to protect it. This is one reason that sometimes even nondemocratic countries can be quite free, even more free than democratic ones. If a powerful enough dictator or single party embarks upon the protection of individual rights, as some do (especially as regards the operations of a free market capitalist system), apart from the lack of political liberty there can be plenty of liberty in such a country. But usually this will not work without majority support. So, where democracy is crucial to liberty is in providing liberty with adequate backing so those who would want to engage in oppression have no chance to do so. In short, it is at the founding of a country—which can be brought about gradually or by revolution—that democracy is crucial. What the limits of such democratic procedure come to is plain: they must address the defense or protection of individual rights by setting up a constitution or similar political order and by giving it firm support, in which the unalienable rights of individuals are fully secure.

Fine, but then what? Where does democracy come in during the administration of a free country? Actually, it does so only in specific, limited areas. For example, democracy is vital in the selection of the system's administrators, in deciding on who will be the political and legal administrators who carry out the task of rights protection (which can be very complicated once the system is in operation in a developed, modern society). Also, more importantly than this, democracy would function in the decision making process that extends the basic principles of a free society to new areas of concern, such as how property rights or rights to free expression apply to, say, radio, television, computer programs, space, and the Internet. Here is where the democratic process would function creatively, lending support to new laws, either through the operations of the courts (via jury verdicts) or the acts of the legislature, kept in check by the judiciary, which would have, in a free society, the job of striking down decisions that violate the rights of individuals.

A free country is one the members of which do not have burdens to which they have not given their full consent imposed upon them by others. Burdens and benefits that arise from nature—say, respectively, a weak constitution or a beautiful figure—do not constitute a limitation on one's liberty, since they (a) were not imposed by others and (b) others have no enforceable obligation to remove these unless they are one's parents or guardians or ones who have contracted to provide such a service (e.g., an insurance company or a hospital).

If a democratic system addresses the ways in which the principle of liberty is upheld effectively enough, there is no conflict between democracy and liberty. But once democracy serves to usurp individual liberty—for example, by leading the majority of voters to trample on others' rights—it is no longer a part of a country's free institutions but becomes, as it has in so many societies around the globe, including in the United States of America, an instrument of greater or lesser tyranny, the proverbial tyranny of the majority.

Duncan spends some time exploring the specifics of a democratic electoral system; I will not address his efforts, since they are all predicated on his conception of a broader than just scope of democracy. For those who consider a constitutional system with demands on everyone to respect individual rights as the proper one, democracy's scope would need to be limited to electing various administrators who will uphold law that rests on such individual rights and on legislators who will develop basic principles to cover novel problems. For example, the principle of the individual's right to freedom of speech and religious worship may need interpretation for what at some point would be novel cases, such as use of the Internet or cell phone communication, and religious practices such as those introduced by the Reverend Moon (who performs mass marriages among the faithful). Beyond electing those who would carry out such a function, all in support of assisting in the maintenance of justice as per the basic constitutional tenets, democracy has no place in a free society (other than when private social groups freely and voluntarily elect to practice democratic methods to reach decisions among their members).[14]

As Duncan reports, "The account of human freedom central to democratic liberalism focuses on people's ability to give shape to their own lives" (p. 100). Is this, however, the right account of human freedom? Certainly there are conceptions of freedom that focus on our ability. One may win some cash and exclaim, "Now I am free to travel to visit all the places where I couldn't go before"; or, "Finally, I am free to help out the causes I wasn't able to support in the past"; or, again, "At last I am free to get my fitness program under way at a proper gym where I can now obtain good advice."

Are these, however, matters of politics? No, not if human beings are treated as moral agents, free to make their own moral decisions regarding how their own lives and resources—including their labor and the compensation they have received for it—are to be allocated by them. Even such issues as racial discrimination are arguably mainly ethical in their nature, not political, unless the discrimination occurs within the processes of the administration of laws. In the latter cases, racial or any other type of discrimination based on factors irrelevant to one's citizenship would amount to administrative injustice. However, if I discriminate for reasons of race or sex in my market transactions—say, I refuse to patronize a shop at the mall because the clerks there are women or black or have some other attributes that are irrelevant to their performance as clerks—I am doing something most likely to be morally wrong but not violating anyone's rights. No one has a right to my patronage. I am not to be conscripted to become a customer of anyone's services, to become anyone's trading partner. To endorse coercing people to be such customers or providers amounts to the promotion of involuntary servitude, except when prior announcement of nondiscriminatory provisions has been made.[15]

Because Duncan's approach to politics heavily relies on the institution of taxation, an institution avidly defended by several prominent political and legal theorists in our time,[16] it will be of some use here to offer some critical comments on that institution. Since the American revolution, when monarchy was rejected by the founders of what came closest to a free society and when sovereignty was legally established for individual human beings, not governments, there has been a problem with taxation. To put it plainly, the institution is an anomaly in a genuinely free society.

In such a society one has unalienable—meaning, never justifiably violable—rights to life, liberty, and the pursuit of happiness, among other rights.[17] But instead of transforming public finance from a coercive to a voluntary system, the framers left taxation intact, albeit changed so that at least there would be representation in the process and it would be limited to support certain clearly public purposes.

Those who cherish government intervention in human social and economic affairs and prize that over individual sovereignty have made use of this anomalous feature of our legal system to justify the expansive state. It is quite natural that this should have occurred—whenever one compromises a principle, eventually the compromise devours the principle altogether. (This is why ethics counsels even against little white lies—they corrupt character.)

By now the tax system in the United States does not even adhere to the principle "No taxation without representation." (It was the famous pre-Revolutionary patriot James Otis who said, "Taxation without representation is tyranny.") Government actually taxes, by means of heavy borrowing, members of future generations, ones certainly not represented in Congress. Taxes are imposed on travelers all over by local politicians who do not represent them. What is far worse, but to be expected, given the logic of such processes, is that instead of confining taxation to financing the only proper function of government, which is "to secure [our] rights," taxation is now used to fund every project in society that the human imagination can conceive.

But, it might be objected, to quote Justice Oliver Wendell Holmes Jr., that "taxation is the price we pay for civilization"? No, and it is useful to consider the source of this idea: It comes from one of America's legal giants who had no sympathy at all for limited government—quite the opposite.

In fact, taxation is best conceived now as a type of extortion. The government tells the citizenry, "You may work for a living only if you hand over roughly 40 percent of your earnings to us to fund goals we have decided need funding. You may live in your home provided you hand over a substantial amount of funds with which we will do what the majority of voters and their representatives believe needs doing." This is not what citizens of a bona fide free society deserve from their agents, ones who are entrusted with protecting, not attacking, their rights.

But, did "we" not enter into a social compact that resulted in the tax system we have? No we didn't, not if we indeed have unalienable rights—no contract can give up anyone's rights. I certainly may not enter a contract the provisions of which include that your rights are violated. A contract—or compact—can only be entered into voluntarily; unwilling third parties may not be conscripted to it.[18] If, as in the case of the closest to a free country in the modern era, namely, the United States, the society is supposed to be grounded on unalienable individual rights, the only way government can come about is through "the consent of the governed." While this had been understood too loosely in the past, even by the American founders, its meaning is clear: You and I must consent to be governed.[19]

Now, we do consent to being governed if we remain within the legal jurisdiction of a certain sphere, but only to the extent that is just; it is the just powers of government only to which we can consent, and to tax is not one of the just powers of government. To be properly funded, some other, but in any case voluntary, means must be found. Since, however, this is a very novel idea—about as novel even in the United States as free markets are in the former Soviet bloc countries or freedom of religion in Iran—studies as to how to bring it off are in short supply. (Remember, most universities are tax funded, so they are not likely to encourage alternative ways of funding government.)

Still, there has been some progress in the study of funding government without any coercive means. One method proposed is to charge for all contracts that are, ultimately, backed by the courts. Certainly, one can just shake hands and proceed, but this is not likely when multimillions are at stake and legal recourse is wanted in case of some kind of mishap. There is also the possibility of funding government via lotteries.[20] At the beginning, governments could make ample money so as to fund plenty of their proper undertakings by selling off all the properties that they should not own in the first place.

These observations do not exhaust the field of public finance for a government of a free society. Still, if the idea were not dismissed so readily by those who prefer taxing their fellows for projects of their own, human beings could put their minds to the task profitably enough and find a way to eliminate this anomaly from our midst.[21] Duncan, unfortunately, sees little worth exploring here, probably because democratic liberals (which, to be sure, is the same as democratic socialists) find the idea of a free society as per the libertarian's understanding of it quite unpalatable.[22]

There are several other details one could take up in Duncan's defense of his democratic liberal polity. There is the complaint that free markets do not actually reward those who deserve being rewarded; that CEOs get a great deal more money than others, and perhaps not always because they deserve it; that there needs to be a government imposed minimum wage, etc.; and so forth. All these measures, many of which are already part of the welfare states of many Western countries, are objectionable from the point of view of the libertarian alternative wherein all forced, nonconsensual exchanges are banned.

Some of the concerns about free markets have to do with the historical fact that the system has always been in force as a mere shadow of its theoretical self, incorporating various elements of feudalism, mercantilism, the welfare state, and other systems that arguably generated the problems—for example, the Great Depression, which can be traced to monetary policies of the federal government.[23]

There is one area of concern, however, that deserves special mention. It has to do with the nature of corporate commerce and, more specifically, the structure of the modern business corporation. First of all, the libertarian theory does not sanction any kind of corporate welfare—subsidies, price supports, protectionism, or the like. All of these would be banned in a free society. Second, the system of limited liability would have to be seriously rethought, partly because it was established under mercantilism and feudalism and, as with taxation, a good deal of it is antithetical to a bona fide free polity. Third, even the practice of silent ownership, without any liability for mal-practice that injures innocent third parties, would need to be reconsidered in a fully free society. By no means, then, is the libertarian lobbying for any special privileges for business, any more than for art, science, education, athletics, entertainment, or any other group of citizens with specific goals they wish to pursue. To the extent that Duncan is critical of libertarianism because he believes it aims to plead a special case for business, he is seriously misunderstanding the position.

In conclusion, I wish to offer some points concerning the general approach taken by those who, like Duncan, see liberty in the tradition exemplified by, among others, Amartya Sen,[24] namely, as enablement rather than absence of coercion or physical intervention in the lives of others. This tradition has been influenced by philosophical positions outside political philosophy proper. The very idea of "liberalism" has been un-der the influence of the modern materialist view that human beings are moved to behave as they do by forces outside their own control, that they lack free will and, therefore, meaning-ful moral responsibility. Accordingly, the very idea of deserv-ing what one obtains through one's conduct and interaction with others has had serious problems. John Rawls made it very clear that the notion of deserving something is difficult if not impossible to support. As he put the point, "No one de-serves his greater natural capacity nor merits a more favorable starting point in society." Why? Because even "a person's character [i.e., the virtues he or she practices that may provide him with ways of getting ahead of others] depends in large part upon fortunate family and social circumstances for which he can claim no credit."[25]

When one views human beings along such lines and also takes them to possess dignity, which warrants treating them with respect, the result is that one regards them as all in the same boat, as it were, socially, economically, psychologically, and so forth. Anyone who is not enjoying reasonable benefits in life is then considered as somewhat of a member of a team to whom considerations are owed by other team members regardless of performance. Whatever misfortune or even failing befalls a person is everyone's responsibility to remedy.

Of course, there is a serious paradox here. The first part of the story, as Rawls and others tell it, removes moral responsibility for human life, but the second part imposes moral responsibility on everyone to take care of all those who have been left deprived. This result is, actually, a problem with modern materialist philosophy, one to which Immanuel Kant tried to provide a solution with his separation of reality into the phenomenal and the noumenal parts—the one behaving entirely deterministically, the other containing, somewhat mysteriously, elements of moral freedom and responsibility.

Democratic liberalism has followed this paradoxical approach in the area of political economy, by making some room for the negative freedom that is required by our moral nature, as well as affirming the propriety of positive freedom that will enable the many who are deemed unable to cope to make headway in life.

In essence, then, the natural law libertarian subscribes to a different human ontology from Duncan's—people are nearly always capable of making responsible choices and need the room in their communities to do this, and only very rare cases warrant departing from this understanding of human social affairs (comparable to how in the criminal law only rarely are defendants exculpated because they are deemed incapable of lawful conduct). This, more than anything else, accounts for why the libertarian alternative is found wanting by many, even while some elements of it are readily incorporated into opposition views.

I wish to end with a point about practicality. Most libertarians realize that despite the fact that theirs is the least utopian of political viewpoints (since it can never promise full solution of all social problems via political means), it is not likely to be fully realized. They take the libertarian political position as the best one available to people, just as a moral philosopher would take the ethics he or she has found justified as the best moral system. But neither expects the system to be lived up to fully, despite the fact that that is what should happen. As with the best ethics, so with the best politics—all one can do is strive to promote it. It would be foolish, knowing about the human proclivity to yield to many temptations to be less than excellent, to expect the best polity to be realized with any regularity.

Notes

1. John Rawls, *A Theory of Justice* (Cambridge, Mass.: Harvard University Press, 1971).

2. John Rawls, *Political Liberalism* (New York: Columbia University Press, 1993).

3. W. Somerset Maugham, *A Writer's Notebook* (Baltimore: Penguin, 1967), 325.

4. Ernest W. Pettifer, *Punishments of Former Days* (East Ardsley, U.K.: EP, 1974), 35–36.

5. For a more detailed account of this point, see Tibor R. Machan, "Human Dignity and the Law," *DePaul Law Review* 26 (1977): 119–26.

6. See, for more of my own libertarian approach—but one developed from a neo-Aristotelian naturalist ethical based—Tibor R. Machan, *Putting Humans First: Why We Are Nature's Favorite* (Lanham, Md.: Rowman & Littlefield, 2004).

7. See an especially focused paper on this topic from Professor Nussbaum: Martha Nussbaum, "Human Functioning and Social Justice: In Defense of Aristotelian Essentialism," *Political Theory* 20 (1992): 202–46.

8. Arguably Duncan builds into his understanding of society the question-begging element of the requirement of choice—cooperation of the membership. Clearly, innumerable societies, ordinarily understood, lack this element.

9. For an elaboration of this point, see Tibor R. Machan, "Why Agreement Is Not Enough," *Philosophia* 28 (2000): 269–81.

10. It is valuable here to recall that there are certain libertarian hints even in Aristotle, as far as what may count for a just society, as when he notes that "the virtues are modes of choice or involve choice." (*Nicomachean Ethics*, 1106a3 & 4.) This suggests that for Aristotle only a polis wherein choice is respected and protected can qualify as encouraging moral virtue since only in such a polis can "modes of choice" be made secure. For more on this way of

reading Aristotle, see Fred D. Miller Jr., *Nature, Justice, and Rights in Aristotle's Politics* (Oxford, U.K.: Oxford University Press, 1995).

11. As an additional small but not negligible matter, Duncan uses "liberal" in the unique contemporary, post New Deal American, sense of that term. "Liberal" had, of course, meant anyone who championed liberty in the sense that one ought to be free from other people's intrusiveness, from oppression or rule by others (monarchs, tsars, dictators, and others who aspire to rule unwilling subjects). The meaning of "liberal" changed for a variety of reasons, not the least of which is that in American calling oneself a social democrat or democratic socialist simply did not meet with open arms. In Europe, in contrast, liberals are still viewed as mostly *classical liberals*, guided by the thought of John Locke, Adam Smith, John Stuart Mill, and Lord Acton.

12. Fareed Zakaria, *The Future of Freedom: Illiberal Democracy at Home and Abroad* (New York: W. W. Norton, 2003). Zakaria, of course, does not advance a radical libertarian case here, although arguably he intimates one.

13. Considering that billions of people around the world, even today, are barred from taking part in any sort of political process, to which they clearly have a basic, natural right (given that everyone has such a right to liberty of action, including political action), it is no surprise that democracy means for them the crux of political liberty. But as Zakaria and others, including John Locke, warned, liberty may be endangered by democracy, despite democracy exemplifying liberty in a certain sphere of human activity. If democracy means the right of all citizens to take part in the political process, there is still the issue of what counts as political. If the scope of politics is minimal, as in the libertarian framework, that may mean that all may vote on certain limited issues. For more, see Tibor R. Machan, *Private Rights and Public Illusions* (New Brunswick, N.J.: Transaction Books, 1995).

14. For the details of the sort of legal order I am sketching here, see Randy R. Barnett, *Restoring the Lost Constitution: The Presumption of Liberty* (Princeton, N.J.: Princeton University Press, 2004).

15. For more on this, see Tibor R. Machan and James E. Chesher, "Capitalism and Racial Justice,"*A Primer on Business Ethics* (Lanham, Md.: Rowman & Littlefield, 2003), chap. 6.

16. See, for example, Liam Murphy and Thomas Nagel, *The Myth of Ownership, Taxes and Justice* (New York: Oxford University Press, 2002), and Stephen Holmes and Cass R. Sunstein, *The Cost of Rights: Why Liberty Depends on Taxes* (New York: W. W. Norton, 1999).

17. The Bill of Rights includes the Ninth Amendment in order to make clear that not only enumerated rights ought to be respected and protected in a free society.

18. An exception would be a compact involving children and their parents. For more on this, see Tibor R. Machan, "Between Parents and Children," *Journal of Social Philosophy* 23 (1992): 16–22.

19. Barnett, *Restoring the Lost Constitution*.

20. For an extensive discussion of funding a legal order without coercion, see Tibor R. Machan, "Dissolving the Problem of Public Goods: Financing Government without Coercive Measures," in *The Libertarian Reader*, ed. T. R. Machan (Lanham, Md.: Rowman & Littlefield, 1982).

21. Considering that much of the research on public finance is carried out at universities and colleges that rely very heavily on the institution of taxation, it is not a mere possibility that those conducting the research have a special interest in not exploring the option being proposed by classical liberals and libertarians. If business corporations can be accused of biased research because of their commitment to making a profit, it is no stretch to assume that state funded education and scholarly institutions will exhibit bias in how they explore possible alternatives to taxation for purposes of public finance.

22. If palatability were the standard for considering an idea worthy of examination, hardly any of the most challenging political systems would pass the test.

23. For discussions of this particular historical event that is often blamed on free market capitalism, see Murray N. Rothbard, *America's Great Depression* (Princeton, N.J.: Van Nostrand, 1963); Milton Friedman and Anna Jacobson Schwartz, *The Great Contraction, 1929–1933*, 1st ed. (Princeton, N.J.: Princeton University Press, 1965); Gene Smiley, *Rethinking the Great Depression* (Chicago: I. R. Dee, 2002); and Jim Powell, *FDR's Folly* (New York: Crown Forum, 2003).

24. Amartya Sen, *Rationality and Freedom* (Cambridge, Mass.: Harvard University Press, 2003).

25. Rawls, *A Theory of Justice*, 104.

6

Democratic Liberalism Defended

Craig Duncan

I am grateful for Professor Machan's critique of my essay on behalf of democratic liberalism. The points he raises merit replies; that is the purpose of my final contribution in this chapter. In particular I will reply to Professor Machan's charges relating to the role of moral intuition, to the scope of democracy, to the nature of political freedom, and to the alleged libertarianism of America's "founding fathers."

1. On Moral Intuition

Quoting Somerset Maugham, Machan alleges that moral intuitions are too insecure a foundation on which to erect a political philosophy. His own theory, Machan claims, rests not on intuition but on a foundation of shared human nature from which his libertarian principles are derivable (pp. 128–29). This, he says, is the method of the natural rights/natural law tradition. I beg to differ, for a number of reasons. First, we should note that there is at least as much diversity of opinion within the natural rights/natural law tradition as there is in the tradition of egalitarian liberalism in which I work. Aristotle, Cicero,

Aquinas, Locke, and all the rest of the thinkers associated with this tradition hardly speak with one voice. Indeed, Machan himself recognizes the diversity of practices that were once thought "natural" but no longer are (p. 128). I do not know why he thinks this diversity is a problem for my theory but not his; after all, it is *his* theory, not mine, that purports to be a "natural" law/rights theory.

Second, Machan's claim to derive ethical principles directly from human nature is implausible, because human nature is itself a mixed bag, with some good elements and some bad elements. We probably have built-in tendencies toward sympathy with and respect for other people, and these are good tendencies. But we probably also have some built-in tendencies to classify people as "insiders" and "outsiders" and to treat the latter group worse. We probably have built-in susceptibilities to superstitious thinking—and so on. Thus one needs moral judgment to distinguish between the good and bad elements of human nature. Once we recognize this, we can see that Machan is doing essentially the same thing as I am. Like me, he is fixing his attention on the unique human capacity for choice and judging that this is a capacity that is worthy of respect. We differ in what this respect amounts to, but this is a substantive difference in our moral views. It is not an epistemological difference in which I rely on "intuition" and he does not.

Third, in his chapter in defense of libertarianism (chapter 1), Machan himself concedes the need for moral *judgment* when it comes to applying his principles. Libertarianism, he there states, is "not a rigid, deductive system of implied public policies" (p. 18). He compares the art of applying political theory with the art of applying medical knowledge, which requires much uncodifiable judgment in particular situations. All of this is true and wise and to Machan's credit. But it flies in the face of his criticisms of my theory. For I need not appeal to "intuition," if this is mysteriously thought of as a faculty by which we gain insight into a rational realm of moral truths that exist in some Platonic heaven. Instead my appeal is to people's capacity for moral judgment, a capacity that develops as their moral experience increases. To my readers I say: Use your best judgment in deciding whose theory better respects the human capacity for choice, mine or Professor Machan's.

Fourth, Machan in fact needs to rely on moral judgment, not just as regards applying his libertarian principles, but even as regards defining the content of the principles themselves. Machan, for instance, recognizes a right of self-defense (pp. 6, 9). Surely, though, this is only a right to take *reasonable* measures in my own defense. If I learn that Harry the Hit Man intends to kill me next week, for instance, I do not have the right to shoot him today as he eats his Big Mac in peace, in a preemptive attack. By contrast, if Harry is swinging a knife at me at close quarters this very moment, then I do have the right to defend myself with lethal force. In the spectrum of cases between these two extremes, however, where exactly do we draw the line between reasonable and unreasonable uses of force? It is not always an easy line to draw; often much judgment is required.[1]

Much the same is true of other libertarian principles. Libertarians will have to distinguish between recklessness (as in reckless driving, say) that rises to the level of criminal negligence and recklessness that falls short of this level—and likewise with other elements of liability law. A key criterion in drawing these lines will be whether or not a person has taken *reasonable* precautions against harming others. Even Machan's beloved property rights will be subject to judgments of reasonableness, moreover, for the degree of control that one has over one's legal property should surely not be absolute. If I live near neighbors, for instance, the fact that I own my front yard does not mean I should be able to play my trumpet on it at three AM, or burn bonfires on it, or have afternoon sex with my partner on it, or fence it in and raise smelly pigs on it, or host bare-knuckled fighting competitions on it, or some other such thing. Accommodating the reasonable demands of others is a necessary element of life in society, and plausible principles of property must recognize this. Drawing the line between reasonable and unreasonable demands, though, requires moral judgment. I cannot see that the task of drawing this line is any less "intuitive" than the task, say, of drawing the line between fair and unfair levels of economic opportunity—a line that my theory regards as important.[2]

2. On Democracy

According to Professor Machan, my defense of democratic liberalism is guilty of "ignoring the most important problem with democracy, namely, its proneness to be illiberal" (p. 130). Moreover, I "fail to raise a most important question, namely, about the *proper scope* of either direct or representative democracy" (p. 131). But in fact I devoted an entire section of chapter 4 to a discussion of individual rights (namely, section 4, "The Dignity-Based Conception of Rights"). When entrenched in a constitution, these rights will limit the authority of democratic legislators. Thus it is hardly the case that according to my theory democratic authority is boundless.[3]

It is true that the individual rights that my theory recognizes are not as expansive as the rights that Machan's libertarian theory recognizes. But this is a strength of my theory, not a weakness, for Machan's theory *excessively* constrains the authority of democratically elected legislators. According to Machan, legislators' authority is restricted to crafting laws that apply libertarian principles to novel situations—say, defining property rights as regards software programs, genetically engineered plants, and so on. In his own words: "Beyond electing those who would carry out such a function [i.e., applying libertarian principles to new situations], all in support of assisting in the maintenance of justice as per the basic constitutional tenets, democracy has no place in a free society" (p. 134). Instead, whenever legislators veer away from libertarian principles, their laws will be voided by a libertarian judiciary tasked with "the job of striking down decisions that violate the rights of individuals" (p. 133).

In other words, in Machan's ideal "free society" libertarianism is not up for debate. If you are not a libertarian, too bad; you still only get to vote for legislators who must operate within the stringently defined boundaries set by libertarian judges. Do you think there should be minimum-wage legislation? Machan's ideal judges will strike it down, if you manage to get such legislation passed. Do you think there should be environmental regulation? Machan's ideal judges will strike it down, if you manage to get it passed. Do you think there should be anti-discrimination legislation? Machan's ideal judges will strike it down, if you manage to get it passed. And so on. Machan's "free society" is actually a society ruled by an elite corps of libertarian judges, who have the final say on virtually every piece of legislation.

That is not the case in the democratic liberal society I envision. It is true that the judiciary will rule out *some* possible laws; legislators cannot ban synagogues, or censor political debate, or stop African Americans from voting, etc. But there will be much democratic debate over tax legislation, environmental regulations, corporate law, minimum-wage legislation, property rights, health care, education policy, campaign finance, and so on. On my theory, policy in these areas is to be set by elected legislators, rather than unelected judges. If you have views on these matters—indeed, if you have *libertarian* views on these matters—then you can vote for politicians who support your views, or you can run for office yourself. Surely this is a fairer way of resolving disagreements in politics than Machan's way of restricting legislators only to debating the best way of applying his own theory. Libertarians' excessive truncation of democracy is thus yet one more instance of their regrettable blindness to the importance of fairness.

3. On Freedom and Discrimination

Machan objects to my understanding of freedom in terms of people's ability to give shape to their lives. He concedes that there are coherent conceptions of freedom that focus on a person's abilities to choose; as he notes, after winning some cash you may exclaim, "Finally, I am free to help out the causes I wasn't able to support in the past." Or, "At last I am free to get my fitness program under way at a proper gym where I can now obtain good advice" (p. 134). However, Machan goes on to deny the political relevance of conceptions of freedom that focus on ability. Indeed, we can agree with the concrete examples he cites. Government should not worry about whether you have a superb personal trainer or about whether you are able to give to as many charities as you would wish.

Other examples, however, reveal that ability-based conceptions of freedom are often politically relevant. Imagine for instance a cancer-stricken person in the 1960s learning of the passage of Medicaid legislation creating government-funded health care for the poor. "Finally," the person might say, "I am free to get treatment for my leukemia, which so far I haven't been able to afford on my wages as a hotel maid." Or imagine an African-American teenager, full of dreams, on the passage of the 1964 Civil Rights Act banning racial discrimination in employment. "At last," she thinks to herself, "I am free to escape the poverty in which I was raised." Are these gains in freedom really politically irrelevant? Should we really say, as Machan must, that while health care and the absence of discrimination increase freedom on *some* conceptions of freedom, these conceptions are not ones that matter for politics? Surely not. For recall that both Machan's libertarianism and my democratic liberalism claim to be founded on an ideal of respect for the unique human capacity of choice. How then can it always be politically irrelevant what people are actually able to choose?

Machan makes it quite clear, however, that abilities to choose are indeed politically irrelevant on his view, even when a person's abilities to choose are limited by racial discrimination. He writes: "Even such issues as racial discrimination are arguably mainly ethical in their nature, not political, unless the discrimination occurs within the processes of the administration of laws" (p. 135). By way of illustrating this point, he notes, "If I discriminate for reasons of race or sex in my market transactions—say, I refuse to patronize a shop at the mall because the clerks there are women or black or have some other attributes that are irrelevant to their performance as clerks—I am doing something most likely to be morally wrong but not violating anyone's rights" (ibid.).

Regarding our economic decisions as consumers, Machan may well be right. But change the example to our economic decisions as *employers* (an example that Machan does not explicitly consider), and things look different: "If I discriminate for reasons of race or sex in my market transactions—say, I refuse to hire any blacks or women in my law firm or factory—I am doing something most likely to be morally wrong, not, however, violating anyone's rights." This is far less plausible. After all, my economic power as an employer is often much, much greater than my economic power as a consumer (for I am just one of thousands or even millions of consumers). As such, it *is* of public concern when as an employer I use my power over others in a discriminatory way, a way that fails to respect the dignity of those others. This is not typically the case with the much less concentrated sort of power that consumers possess.

These reflections reveal that libertarians' rejection of anti-discrimination employment legislation is a serious flaw. More needs saying, though, for some people will agree with libertarians' rejection of anti-discrimination legislation, on the alleged grounds that racial discrimination is no longer a significant phenomenon in the U.S. economy. In response to such people, two points are in order. First, it is important to note that libertarians do not just oppose anti-discrimination laws in contemporary America; they oppose it at all times and all places. So to African Americans living in the Jim Crow South prior to the civil rights era, libertarians could say only, "We will dismantle laws that legally *require* discrimination. But we will not pass laws *forbidding* discrimination by business owners and employees. If you don't want a person to discriminate against you, then talk to him or her and convince him or her of the wrongness of discrimination."

Is this enough? No doubt eradicating legally required discrimination is necessary. But it is not enough. Writing in 1955, the eminent historian C. Van Woodward observed,

> Right here it is well to admit, and even to emphasize, that *laws are not an adequate index to the extent and prevalence of segregation and discrimination practices in the South.* The practices often anticipated and sometimes exceeded the laws. It may be confidently assumed—and it could be verified by present observation—that there is more Jim Crowism practiced in the South than there are Jim Crow laws on the books.[4]

In other words, Jim Crow laws often merely ratified in law various practices that already existed and were able to sustain themselves without the law. Hence merely dismantling the laws is not enough. And this is one example of many. Consider too how sex discrimination in the past went well beyond whatever sex discrimination the law required.[5] Consider as well the case of modern India, where caste discrimination continues to exist in ample measure despite not being required by law.[6] To a low-caste individual who calls for a legal ban on caste discrimination, a libertarian like Machan can only say, "No, sorry, such legal action would be unjust; it must not be done." "But caste itself is gravely unjust!" the individual will likely—and rightly—retort.

The second point in response to critics of anti-discrimination law is this: It is unfortunately not the case that in the United States racial discrimination is a thing of the past. The most convincing evidence of continuing job discrimination comes from "audit studies," in which black and white testers are given resumes identical in terms of education and job qualifications; they then apply for jobs, go for interviews, etc., and in the process differences of treatment are noted. In a dramatic recent study, sociologist Devah Pager had four college-educated testers, two black and two white, apply to 350 entry-level jobs in the Milwaukee area. Their qualifications were designed to be the same, with the one exception that within each black pair and each white pair one of the testers reported that he had spent eighteen months in prison for cocaine possession. Alarmingly, the white tester who reported a criminal record was *more* likely to be called for an interview (called back 17 percent of the time) than was the black tester with *no* criminal record (called back 14 percent of the time).[7] Simply being black is apparently more of a liability in the current job market than is being a convicted felon.

Other studies back up these results. Economists Marianne Bertrand and Sendhil Mullainathan, for example, recently sent out five thousand résumés to 1,300 employers advertising job openings in Boston and Chicago. The résumés were constructed to be identical in quality, the one difference being that the names on some were black-sounding names like "Jamal" and "Lakisha," whereas the names on others were white-sounding names like "Emily" and "Greg." Disturbingly, applicants with white-sounding names were 50 percent more likely to be called for interviews than were those with black-sounding names.[8] These studies and others[9] reveal a continued need for anti-discrimination law.[10]

4. On Libertarianism and the "Founding Fathers"

Machan spends a good portion of his critique reaffirming his opposition to taxation. In my critique of libertarianism in chapter 2, I said why Machan is wrong to think that taxation is always unjust, no matter the type or amount of taxation. Rather than repeat those points here, I want instead to comment on Machan's attempt to link his opposition to taxes with the views of America's founding fathers.

As he did in his defense of libertarianism in chapter 1, Machan in his critique of my view appeals to the Declaration of Independence, written by Thomas Jefferson—in particular, to its mention of the unalienable rights to "life, liberty and the pursuit of happiness" (p. 135; cf. pp. 4, 5, 28). Machan interprets this phrase as supporting his own libertarian conception of rights. Jefferson and other founding fathers did not interpret it this way, however; Machan admits this himself when he notes (p. 136) that the founders opposed not taxation in general as he does but rather taxation *without representation*.[11] In fact, Jefferson's choice in the Declaration to speak of "life, liberty, and *the pursuit of happiness*" rather than the Lockean threesome of "life, liberty, and *property*," is itself significant. Remarkably, when the Marquis de Lafayette, the statesman and principal author of the French 1789 Declaration of the Rights of Man and Citizens, sent Jefferson a draft of this document and invited him to comment upon it, Jefferson returned it with the words "right to property" bracketed and replaced by "pursuit of happiness."[12] For Jefferson, property rights were important, but important mainly as instruments for the promotion of human happiness; when property law stands in the way of human happiness, it is in need of reform.

Other writings of Jefferson confirm the instrumental view he took of property rights. In an important letter to James Madison, for instance, Jefferson pens a passage that is worth quoting at length:

> I am conscious that an equal division of property is imprac-
> ticable. But the consequences of this enormous inequality
> producing so much misery to the bulk of mankind, legisla-
> tors cannot invent too many devices for subdividing prop-
> erty, only taking care to let their subdivisions go hand in
> hand with the natural affections of the human mind. The de-
> scent of property of every kind therefore to all the children,
> or to all the brothers and sisters, or other relations in equal
> degree is a politic measure, and a practicable one. Another
> means of silently lessening the inequality of property is to
> exempt all from taxation below a certain point, and to tax
> the higher portions of property in geometrical progression
> as they rise. Whenever there is in any country, uncultivated
> lands and unemployed poor, it is clear that the laws of prop-
> erty have been so far extended as to violate natural right.
> The earth is given as a common stock for man to labour and

live on. If, for the encouragement of industry we allow it to be appropriated, we must take care that other employment be furnished to those excluded from the appropriation.[13]

While Jefferson here recognizes that strict equality is not an achievable goal, he clearly approves of measures to reduce inequality, including progressive taxation and public employment for those who cannot find work.

We can also note non-libertarian views among other influential thinkers at the time of the founding of the United States.[14] Benjamin Franklin, for instance, takes a line nearly identical to the line I defend in chapter 2, writing that:

all the property that is necessary to a Man, for the Conservation of the Individual and the Propagation of the Species, is his natural Right, which none can justly deprive him of: But all Property superfluous to such purposes is the Property of the Publick, who, by their Laws, have created it, and who may therefore by other laws dispose of it, whenever the Welfare of the Publick shall demand such Disposition. He that does not like civil Society on these Terms, let him retire and live among Savages. He can have no right to the benefits of Society, who will not pay his Club towards the Support of it.[15]

Sounding a similar note, Thomas Paine, the author of the famous pamphlet *Common Sense* (which probably did more to galvanize support for revolution against Britain than any other piece of colonial writing), writes as follows in his pamphlet *Agrarian Justice* (1797):

Separate an individual from society, and give him an island or a continent to possess, and he cannot acquire personal property. He cannot be rich. So inseparably are the means connected with the end, in all cases, that where the former do not exist the latter cannot be obtained. All accumulation, therefore, of personal property, beyond what a man's own hands produce, is derived to him by living in society; and he owes on every principle of justice, of gratitude, and of civilization, a part of that accumulation back again to society from whence the whole came.[16]

Obviously, Mr. Paine was no libertarian.

I do not mean to charge Machan with wrongly thinking that the founding fathers shared his views on every point. He is surely aware they did not. The passages quoted above, however, should succeed in countering the false impression that Machan creates, namely, that Thomas Jefferson and the other founding fathers shared his basic libertarian foundation but just failed consistently to follow through with its implications in every detail. Moreover, whatever the founding fathers thought, we should of course not defer uncritically to past thinkers, but instead think for ourselves. I am certain Professor Machan would agree. Ironically, so does Thomas Jefferson. I wish to end, then, on a point of agreement, by quoting Jefferson himself:

> But I know also, that laws and institutions must go hand in hand with the progress of the human mind. As that becomes more developed, more enlightened, as new discoveries are made, new truths disclosed, and manners and opinions change with the change of circumstances, institutions must advance also, and keep pace with the times. We might as well require a man to wear still the coat which fitted him when a boy, as civilized society to remain ever under the regimen of their barbarous ancestors.[17]

Notes

1. For some idea of the moral subtleties involved, see Judith Jarvis Thomson, "Self-Defense," *Philosophy and Public Affairs* 20 (1991): 283–310.

2. I explore fairness *via* the notion of desert in section 7 of chapter 4. I mention this here because in his critique in chapter 5 Machan spends a good deal of time (pp. 139ff.) criticizing John Rawls for his attack on notions of desert. Whatever its merits against Rawls, however, this criticism does not impugn *my* defense of democratic liberalism, since far from attacking desert, I showed how notions of desert support democratic liberalism rather than libertarianism. Any theory that allows *luck* as large a role in determin-

ing people's fates as libertarianism does is a theory that assuredly fails to respect claims of desert.

3. Machan also errs interpretively in referring to me as a democratic socialist (p. 138). Socialism is defined as an economic system in which the means of production are publicly owned. I am not convinced that such a system is workable, at least not without unacceptable costs in other values besides fairness. So I am in favor of a regulated capitalist economy, and hence am not a socialist. Perhaps as debates between capitalists and socialists continue, and as socialist models get defended in ever more detail, I will eventually be persuaded. (The most likely contender is David Schweickart's "market socialist" model, which has no capital markets but does have competitive markets for consumer goods and factors of production. See David Schweickart, *After Capitalism* [Lanham, Md.: Rowman and Littlefield, 2002].) For now, though, I see no alternative to some form of capitalism. Fortunately there are many such forms. I favor the form that (as I argue in chapter 4) best respects human dignity.

4. C. Vann Woodward, *The Strange Career of Jim Crow* (Oxford, U.K.: Oxford University Press, 1955), 102 [emphasis in the original]. Quoted in Samuel Freeman, "Illiberal Libertarians: Why Libertarianism Is Not a Liberal View," *Philosophy and Public Affairs* 30 (2001): 135. Freeman argues that libertarianism ought not to be considered even a version of classical liberalism, inasmuch as (among other reasons) it shuns all legal devices for combating castelike privileges—privileges that liberalism from its inception has always opposed.

5. Moreover, sex discrimination still exists. For evidence, see Ian Ayres, *Pervasive Prejudice? Unconventional Evidence of Race and Gender Discrimination* (Chicago: University of Chicago Press, 2003). In speaking of *past* sex discrimination, my point above is that even when sexual discrimination in private employment was as blatant and severe as it was in the past, a libertarian government would have been powerless to do anything about it.

6. For evidence of the reality of caste discrimination in contemporary India, see Human Rights Watch, *Caste Discrimination: A Global Concern* (2001), available online at www.hrw.org/reports/2001/globalcaste/. Sex discrimination is also a large problem in India. On this see Martha Nussbaum, "Sex, Laws, and Inequality: India's Experience," *Daedalus* 131 (2002): 95–106.

7. Devah Pager, "The Mark of a Criminal Record," *American Journal of Sociology* 108 (2002): 937–75.

8. Sendhil Mullainathan and Marianne Bertrand, "Are Emily and Greg More Employable than Lakisha and Jamal? A Field Experiment on Labor Market Discrimination," *American Economic Review* 94 (2004): 991–1013; for a brief summary of their research, see Alan B. Krueger, "Sticks and Stones Can Break Bones, but the Wrong Name Can Make a Job Hard to Find," *New York Times*, December 12, 2002.

9. E.g., Marc Bendick Jr., Charles W. Jackson, and Victor A. Reinoso, "Measuring Employment Discrimination through Controlled Experiments," *Review*

of Black Political Economy 23 (1994): 25–48; Ayres, *Pervasive Prejudice?;* see also the audit studies described in the U.S. Department of Housing and Urban Development, *Housing Discrimination Study 2000,* an executive summary of which is available online at www.huduser.org/Publications/pdf/Phase1_Executive_Summary.pdf.

10. Libertarians sometimes argue that the invisible hand of economic competition can be counted on to eliminate discrimination. This takes too idealized a picture of economic competition. For a persuasive rebuttal, see Cass Sunstein, *Free Markets and Social Justice* (New York: Oxford University Press, 1997), chap. 6.

11. Jefferson writes: "I approved from the first moment of . . . the power of taxation [in the new Constitution]. I thought at first that [it] might have been limited. A little reflection soon convinced me it ought not to be." Letter to Francis Hopkinson (1789), in *The Writings of Thomas Jefferson,* ed. Albert Ellery Bergh (Washington, D.C.: Thomas Jefferson Memorial Association, 1903–1904), 7:300. Quoted at etext.virginia.edu/jefferson/quotations/jeff1330.htm.

12. Richard K. Matthews, *The Radical Politics of Thomas Jefferson* (Lawrence: University Press of Kansas, 1984), 28. This source makes clear how removed Jefferson's political philosophy is in many respects from Machan's libertarianism.

13. Letter to James Madison (October 28, 1785), in *The Papers of Thomas Jefferson,* ed. Julian P. Boyd (Princeton, N.J.: Princeton University Press, 1950–1982), 8:681–82. Quoted at press-pubs.uchicago.edu/founders/documents/v1ch15s32.html.

14. For a helpful overview of the variety of political ideologies that figured in the public debate over ratification of the Constitution, see Isaac Kramnick, "The 'Great National Discussion': The Discourse of Politics in 1787," *William and Mary Quarterly* 45 (1988): 3–32. For a collection of quotations from the founding fathers specifically to do with property, see press-pubs.uchicago.edu/founders/tocs/v1ch16.html. On equality, see press-pubs.uchicago.edu/founders/tocs/v1ch15.html.

15. Benjamin Franklin, Letter to Robert Morris (December 25, 1783), in *The Writings of Benjamin Franklin,* ed. Albert Henry Smyth (New York: Macmillan, 1905–1907), 9:138. Quoted at press-pubs.uchicago.edu/founders/documents/v1ch16s12.html.

16. Paragraph 59 of Thomas Paine, *Agrarian Justice.* An online version of this work is available at www.thomaspaine.org/Archives/agjst.html. In this same work Paine proposed that a national fund be created by a 10 percent tax on inheritances. From this fund would be paid old-age pensions (i.e., social security), as well as grants to young adults to help them get started in the world of work.

17. Thomas Jefferson, letter to Samuel Kercheval (July 12, 1816), in *The Works of Thomas Jefferson,* ed. Paul Leicester Ford (New York: Knickerbocker, 1904), 12:12. Quoted in Matthews, *Radical Politics,* 22.

Index

About the Authors

Craig Duncan is Assistant Professor of Philosophy at Ithaca College in Ithaca, New York.

Tibor R. Machan is R. C. Hoiles Professor of Business Ethics and Free Enterprise at Chapman University in Orange, California.